EVERYT... KNEW YOU WANTED TO KNOW ABOUT DEATH

■ Egyptians sometimes kept a mummified body aboveground for several years, using it as surety to borrow money. Few people re-neged on the deal. If they did, they were refused a burial of their own and forfeited entry to the afterlife.

■ A 1993 survey in the U.S. of women in the workplace found that more secretaries were murdered on the job than police officers and bartenders combined.

■ In 2001 a Romanian smoker made the news by constructing a coffin from discarded cigarette packets. Mihai Cepleuca from Bucharest used seven thousand packets. The retiree, a two-pack-a-day man, plans to be buried in the coffin, which has a pil-low made of filter tips.

■ Urban Myth: Hair and nails don't grow in the coffin—the illu-sion is created by the retraction of the skin.

DEATH*

* A User's Guide

Tom Hickman

Delta Trade Paperbacks

DEATH: A USER'S GUIDE
A Delta Book

PUBLISHING HISTORY
Ebury Press edition published 2002
Delta trade paperback edition / July 2003

Published by
Bantam Dell
A Division of Random House, Inc.
New York, New York

Cataloging in Publication data is on file with the publisher.

ISBN 0-385-33705-1

Manufactured in the United States of America
Published simultaneously in Canada

ROS 10 9 8 7 6 5 4 3 2 1

CONTENTS

CONTENTS

CONTENTS

CONTENTS

INTRODUCTION

 Questions, Questions

"What is the answer?" [silence] "In that case, what is the question?"
    —*last words of novelist Gertrude Stein*

There's an old gag—a play on words—that asks, if the cemetery is a place that nobody wants to go to on a permanent basis, why are people dying to get into it?

On a warm summer's day, with spangled sunshine in the yews and with plots here and there bright with flowers, the tranquil charm of a cemetery seems far removed from its purpose. Children play among the plots, lovers holding hands read the inscriptions on the headstones, aware, no doubt, of death as an abstract proposition but one so far beyond their horizon, it really has nothing to do with them.

The idea becomes less abstract as we grow older, but we rarely think about our own death, except perhaps at a funeral, when we might imagine a tap on the shoulder from the Grim Reaper. He's going to get you one day, of course, even if, vernacularly speaking, you're not dying to let him. However Mediterranean your diet, whatever your intake of omega-3 fish oils and your adherence to an exercise regime, it's off to the six-by-two in the earth, toes pointing to the daisies—unless you choose cremation, as increasing numbers of people do, in which case you'll vanish up the crematorium chimney.

With a bit of luck, when the time comes, you'll think like the twinkle-eyed TV pundit Malcolm Muggeridge, who wrote that the pleasantest thing about old age was that "you wake up in the night and you find that you are half in and half out of your battered old carcass. It seems quite a toss-up whether you go back and resume full occupancy of your mortal body, or make off towards the bright glow you see in the sky."

The truth is out there, but is that glow in the sky a symbol of life after death or just a glow in the sky? The Victorian Orientalist and explorer Sir Richard Burton promised his wife as he lay dying that he'd come back to her, presumably with the answer. He spoke at least seventeen languages, so you'd have thought he could have talked his way around the hereafter, and he had experience of getting in and out of places—disguised as an Indian Pathan, he made the pilgrimage to the forbidden city of Mecca. Lady Burton hung around his mausoleum. He didn't show. Which leaves us with our questions: Is there a heaven? Is there a hell? And where are we individually bound? Or is life merely a dream before extinction, a cradle, as Nabokov suggested, swinging over the void between nothingness and nothingness?

DEATH*

* A User's Guide

RESPECTING THE DEAD

Artifacts for the Afterlife

You can't take it with you, it's said, but for millennia they did. The Neanderthals began the practice of putting goods in graves fifty thousand years ago, give or take the odd ten thousand years. As they were not the hairy, bulbous-browed knuckle-trailers of popular belief but members of the genus *Homo sapiens* with anatomically modern brains, it's reasonable to conjecture that, like the civilizations that followed, they thought that existence continued in some place beyond the grave, that a journey to get there was involved, and that the dead needed a few creature comforts to undertake it and to make the afterlife the good life when they got there.

Not belonging to a consumerist society, the Neanderthals had little to give: food and drink, the odd flintstone ax, fire charcoals. Food, drink, and fire-lighting implements remained the staples in later history, but eating utensils, household items, clothing, and jewelry were added. Different peoples, not surprisingly, reflected their culture in what they considered essential. On a prosaic level, the Arctic Eurasians from Norway to Siberia send off their dead with the reins of a sled, fish, copious amounts of tobacco, and plentiful tallow—the Arctic Circle is generally a gloomy place. More fundamentally maritime races like the Scandinavians, the Anglo-Saxons, and the South Sea Islanders buried their elite dead with their boats, as did the ancient Egyptians, whose world revolved around the sacred Nile. The Twana Indians of the American Northwest seacoast also buried the dead in their canoes, although they placed them in trees. Sometimes the Arctic tribes and the Scandinavians set their dead adrift at sea—alight in the latter case, as the Vikings especially rather liked setting things on fire—emphasizing that a journey was being undertaken.

The practical ancient Greeks (copied by the Romans), assuming that you were likely to have to pay your way in the next world as in this, saw their dead on their way with a coin in their mouths to pay Chiron, the ferryman, who would row them across the river Styx to where they were headed. As a bit of contingency planning the Greeks placed honey cake or bread in the coffin as a bribe to the three-headed dog-demon Cerberus, who guarded the entrance to the underworld. Quite as practical as the Greeks, the Chinese also placed coins in the mouth of the corpse and cakes and bread in the coffin to ward off not Cerberus, but the pack of vicious dogs that awaited the dead—customs continued to this day. But living under a complex and corrupt bureaucracy as they did, and assuming that nothing would be different on the other side, they also placed jade, pearls, and gold leaf in the corpse's mouth. This was to bribe the officials, either in hell to secure their release or in heaven to buy a better class of rebirth on earth. And they still send their dead special paper money, drawn on the Bank of Hell, by burning it. There's a reflection of all this in the British actor Robert Morley asking for his credit cards to be buried with him. After his funeral in 1992 readers of *The Times* pondered in the letters page what they might appreciate most accompanying them on the other side. Heather Tanner of Woodbridge specified a good map. "I have immense trouble finding my way in this life," she wrote, "so I am extremely worried about the next." "A pair of earplugs," specified Sir David Wilcocks of Cambridge, "in case the heavenly choirs, singing everlastingly, are not in tune." Wrote M. L. Evans of Chester: "In the unfortunate event of the miscarriage of justice and several thousand years ensuing before my sentence is quashed, I will take a fire extinguisher."

The prodigious amount of worldly goods that went along with the elite deceased in ages past included not only precious artifacts but also armor, weaponry, chariots, pets, and horses. Everyone knows something of the wealth that accompanied the pharaohs into their tombs, but prodigality was in every culture. In the three-thousand-year-old grave of a Scythian warrior prince and his consort excavated in southern Siberia in 2001, for instance, more than 46 pounds of treasure was discovered, including a solid gold quiver and solid gold goblets and necklaces; the bodies were dressed in garments covered in more than nine thousand pieces of gold.

 ## Living Death for Wives and Servants

From our perspective, what was most distasteful about trying to ensure that dead rulers, nobles, and heroes could continue in the afterlife in the manner to which they had become accustomed was that it also involved truncating the lives of others. In Sumer (the earliest civilization, from about 3500 B.C.) and the other Mesopotamian cultures of Babylonia and Assyria, in ancient Egypt and early Greece, in Scythia, Mongolia, and Turkey, in Scandinavia and China, and among the Celts of central and western Europe, the Central Americans, and numerous African peoples, it was common practice for servants, soldiers, wives, and dependent children to join their master in the grave. Archaeology suggests that anything between six and eighty people were not unusual for a top banana, but often the funerary retinue was in the hundreds. In the fifth century A.D. five hundred mounted warriors had their throats cut and were buried with Attila the Hun; in the ninth, another five hundred warriors went with the Viking chieftain Raknar into his burial ship. Improbably, according to the thirteenth-century Venetian traveler Marco Polo, more than twenty thousand people who saw the body of the Mongol leader Mangu Khan as it went on pilgrimage to burial enjoyed the privilege of joining him permanently.

It seems that many of those dependent on the powerful were happy to make the one-way trip in their company. They were, after all, going to what was hoped to be a better place; their job was to serve; and anyway prevailing thought was that, as they belonged in the most absolute sense to those who had departed this world, they too were already dead to it.

In the classical ancient world women did commit suicide to join their men in the afterlife, and the Roman writer Pomponius Mela observed that among the Celts some wives willingly cast themselves onto the flames of their husbands' funeral pyres. It was a Viking custom too, as it was among Hindu sects in India as late as the nineteenth century. In the same period new widows in New Guinea could elect to be garrotted (as was the Siberian Scythian princess) to accompany their spouses, or buried alive with them—or not, as they choose. In Fiji widows faced the same options but without the "not."

It's hard to believe that in any period or place human beings who were seen as mere accessories of someone else's life got anywhere by saying "Can we talk about this?" While some wives no doubt accepted their fate, the willingness of others is at least questionable. The myths of Greece and Rome suggested that wives considered it an honor and obligation to die with their deceased lord, but mythology is an idealized collection of as-it-ought-to-have-been stories, and as feminist historians have pointed out, the writers of myth and legend were all male. On this subject they may have been economical with the *verité*. As to Viking and Hindu wives and concubines electing the fiery exit, there's evidence that, while the choice was meant to be entirely volun-

BUMPING off the family and the hired help gradually died out with the passing of the centuries. It was prevalent among Egyptians during the Early Dynastic Period that began circa 3100 B.C., but by the time of the Old Kingdom 500 years or so later, they'd decided that images served the same purpose, which must have been a big relief all around.

In Africa today the tradition of sending the wife (or wives), counselors, and slaves along with the chief has been replaced by animal sacrifice—the blood is poured into the grave to fortify the traveler on his way to the other world. Hindus who can afford it also sacrifice an animal, usually a goat (now that sacrificing a cow is forbidden by law), rather than a woman, with the added advantage that the deceased's sins are transferred to it—a scapegoat, no less. The term actually springs from ancient Hebrew ritual in which the same transference of sin was involved—but afterward the goat was allowed to toddle off into the wilderness.

China's first emperor, the despotic Quin Shi Huang (259–210 B.C.), who built the Great Wall, took wives, concubines, ministers, guards, and assorted servants to keep him company in his tomb at Xian. But he was a man who took no chances—he also surrounded himself with 6,000 terracotta warriors, all life size and individually sculptured.

The Chinese, who were still burying all and sundry with dead emperors in the thirteenth century, also changed to surrogates. Just as they burn paper money to send to the deceased, they now burn paper servants.

SUTTEE still plays a role in the cremation of Hindu males, but only a symbolic one. A wife now lies beside her deceased husband on the funeral pyre while the sacred verse is uttered: "Oh mortal, this woman, your wife, wishing to be joined to you in a future world, is lying by your corpse. Always she had observed her duties as your faithful wife, but now grant her your permission to abide in this world of the living." And then she gets off . . . almost always. *Suttee* is alleged occasionally in remote districts.

tary, considerable pressure was brought to bear on them to "do the right thing." The British who governed India in the nineteenth century were appalled by reports that narcotics were administered to prevent women from changing their minds and that sometimes they were tied to the funeral pyres—which hardly indicated free choice. Noting that during the cremation ceremony the music was deliberately played very loudly—a widow's final words were considered prophetic, and it was thought best that what she really said couldn't be heard—the British prohibited the practice of wifely immolation (*suttee* or *sati*, Sanskrit for "virtuous wife") in around 1830, although it took large-scale social reform by succeeding leaders, including Mahatma Gandhi in the first half of the twentieth century, to stop it.

All in all one can only say that the tenth-century Swedish queen Sigridr the Proud had the right idea. She divorced the old king Eric Sigrsaell precisely to avoid going to the grave with him.

Universal Treatment of the Dying

However misguided in our terms other societies have been, one thing remains true: they were doing their best to ensure the postmortem well-being of their dead. Paramount in this was burial or cremation or whatever other means of final disposal was acceptable to the culture. An improper handling of the remains, or none at all, could prevent the dead from making it to their destination—a view strongly held in Egypt, ancient Greece, and Rome; in today's Orthodox Judaism an unburied body is

THROUGHOUT history it's been considered important for the dead to be buried in their homelands. Today Japanese and Chinese sons return the bodies of their parents to Japan and China, sometimes at enormous cost, just as in the West bodies are sent home by air, rail, or boat. Whatever the normal funeral practices of their culture, warriors of every race killed abroad—including crusaders in the Holy Land— preferred to have the flesh boiled off their bones so that these, at least, could be laid to rest in home soil.

an affront to God and to man, and among primitive peoples it causes great concern.

In ancient Greece a general who failed to provide for the burial of the slain—at the very least a mass grave on the field of battle—was held guilty of a capital offense. The Greeks did not refuse burial to an enemy. No one, they thought, should suffer the fate of Odysseus's friend Elpenor who, "unburied and unwept" on the island of Circe, was left a sad shade, trapped between this world and the next. Some peoples, including the Mongols, Turks, and Germanic tribes, frequently left their enemies unburied precisely to inflict this everlasting punishment. The Arctic tribes used to eat the hearts and livers of dead enemies to prevent their resurrection.

Almost without exception throughout history, peoples have believed that the soul or spirit of the dead lingers near the body. To the ancient Egyptians this meant both the *ka*—the dead person's spiritual double—and their *ba*—the human "personality" that remained to go sight-seeing when it wasn't traveling with the sun god. That is why the Egyptians embalmed their dead; the corpse acted as a kind of home base until *ka* and *ba* were reunited with the body in the realm of the dead.

The Zoroastrians in ancient Persia (and the surviving followers of the religion in Iran and the hundred thou-

BECAUSE they believed the body was essential to reach the afterlife, the Egyptians had a particular horror of death by fire, which would have destroyed the spirit's "base." Those they sentenced to death were executed by burning, so that no afterlife was possible. Dying in a foreign land was a risky business afterlife-wise, because a proper burial might be impossible, so the Egyptians tried to bring their dead—or at least their elite dead—home. The records of later foreign expeditions show that as many as thirty embalmers accompanied the army. Once surrogates for the self became acceptable, Egyptian merchants leaving the country carried small stone models of themselves. If they died abroad, these were sent back for proxy burial.

For the Egyptians death by drowning was a most fortunate way to go, especially in the sacred Nile. It meant immediate transportation to the realm of the dead.

sand Parsees in India) believed that the spirit remained for three days after death. In Islam still the spirit is said to watch the rituals and the funeral—a belief also held in contemporary Transylvania and Hungary and not unknown in Catholic Ireland—and to be present in the family home for up to a month and in the grave for up to a year.

The corollary of such belief was that treating the dead with respect had an element of self-protection about it: if the watching just-dead were satisfied with the arrangements, then they wouldn't turn nasty—as they were capable of doing (see Chapter 6). There was also the likelihood that if the departed departed as satisfied customers, they would confer blessings—good luck, prosperity, children—on their descendants. Medieval Europe was an enthusiastic signatory to this idea, as East Asia and much of Africa still are. There was also some insurance: when the time came for your permanent departure, those already gone ahead might just be in a position to put in a good word for you.

Naturally enough, there were and are differences from culture to culture in the way that the dying are treated—in the West, for example, people expect to do their dying in bed, whereas Hindus are taken from their beds and laid on the earth when death is imminent—but the customs and rituals of death are surprisingly similar in whatever time or place. The corpse is washed (it was once commonly held that, polluted by death as it was, it would otherwise be refused entry to the hereafter). This is usually done with water—for Hindus, drawn, if possible, from the Ganges or other sacred river—but not always. The Zoroastrians use cow's urine, while in Africa oil or clarified butter is preferred. In ancient Greece and Rome old women washed and laid out the body, a practice that was prevalent in Western culture until the first half of the twentieth century. Muslim men wash men and women wash women; if a woman must be washed by a male relative, it must be through her clothes. A Muslim who dies among strangers should only be rubbed with sand. Unique to Judaism is that the washing is done by a specialized holy fellowship, the *chevra kadisha.* Washing may be dispensed with for Islamic martyrs (depending on the method of death, there may be no choice), whose martyrdom already purifies them for the afterlife.

 ## Displaying the Deceased

All societies try to have their dead looking their best for their final big day. The ancient Egyptians spent weeks or months on the business (see Chapter 3), stuffing women's breasts (not with silicone implants but with straw, sand, linen, and mud), refashioning nipples from buttons and eyes from obsidian or brass balls, and giving the bodies a nice coat of ochre: red for men, yellow for women. As they virtually took bodies apart in the embalming process, putting them back together with a few add-ons was somewhat necessary. In the modern world, Americans are widely regarded as overdoing similar if infinitely more sophisticated enhancements. In *The American Way of Death,* Jessica Mitford poured scorn on such funerary cosmetic ministrations as eye caps, face formers, denture replacers, lip pinning (smile please), and the injection of facial hollows. "Alas, poor Yorick!" she wrote. "How surprised he would be to see how his counterpart today is whisked off to a funeral parlour and is in short order sprayed, sliced, pierced, pickled, trussed, trimmed, creamed, waxed, painted, rouged and neatly dressed—transformed from a common corpse into a Beautiful Memory Picture." We'll come to the slicing, piercing, and pickling in due course. As to the transformation aspect, not much has changed in the forty years since Mitford's book was first published. At least a dozen U.S. companies offer funerary cosmetics to the trade: "Try Nadene Cover-Up Cosmetics and discover what over 7,000 other funeral directors already know. 100% GUARANTEED ABSOLUTELY RISK FREE." Risk free? To whom, don't you wonder?

The odd cosmetic lick is not unknown in the British way of death, but routinely, nothing more. The British dead are dealt with at the undertaker's, not the funeral parlor—and the British have never been attracted to open casket viewing.

When it comes to what the departed should wear to face the final curtain, some cultures have favored simplicity; most have buried their dead in their finest or in fur; and the elite dead have invariably bowed out in full regalia. Throughout history the shroud has been the commonest covering. This was usually a plain linen winding sheet, tied or sewn at top and bottom, although Europeans in the Middle Ages waxed it to slow decay, called it "cerecloth," and left a hole at the head, to make it easier for the dead to arise at the final judgment. The grave garb of Muslims and Hebrews, the shroud was adopted by the early Christians partially as a protest at the Roman custom of dressing the (elite, male) dead in the pomp of their purple-trimmed togas. The ordinary Jewish shroud is of white muslin; linen is reserved for the priestly classes.

White is the predominant color for the dead (Muslims also permit green), but on the matter of color Western religion is generally indifferent, though the Amish, who don black in their daily life, are buried in white and Mormons in white with a green apron. Most in the West go in their best bib and tucker. Many Americans choose special new burial clothes, and the custom is not unknown in some other cultures, notably among the Chinese, who dress the dead in new garments called "longevity" clothes. Mitford, however, found the practice ridiculous. Special underwear? Special hosiery? Her favorite was the "Fit-a-Fut" one-size-fits-all coffin slipper from the Practical Burial Footwear Company, which saw no irony in that "practi-

IN 1666 (followed by Scotland in 1707) the English government passed a law making it obligatory for shrouds to be of cloth made from wood pulp—a measure to save rag linen for the burgeoning paper industry. In England this saved 200,000lbs of the stuff annually. But the rich who were of a mind still went to the grave in silk—on payment of a fine. As the eighteenth century progressed and coffins became available more widely than to the very rich, shrouds fell out of favor—the more permanent structure of the coffin allowed *à la mode* dressing up.

cal"; even at an open casket viewing the bottom half of the lid is usually closed. Mitford was also tickled by the "post-mortem restoration bra."

In more cultures than not, displaying the dead so that others could pay their respects has been the norm. Putting the body of a dead monarch on display was important throughout history virtually everywhere: as part of the process of succession, the subjects needed to see for themselves that death had happened, especially in medieval times, when representatives of other powers came for the state funeral, political turmoil was in the air, alliances could change, and possibly there might be a grab for the crown. Among Euro-Asiatic, Arctic, African, and Aboriginal Australian peoples, and some Native Americans, the tradition was for the dead not only to be displayed but to be sat up to "eat" with the living and say good-bye; indeed, among the Mambai of Indonesia the corpse stayed seated in the family home until it rotted. Turks left the bodies of esteemed dead in state in their yurts (round tents) for a time and, like the Scythians and Mongols, put a dead king on a wagon and took him on a farewell tour of the tribes he'd ruled.

The problem with transportation or prolonged display, which together could take months, was that the body begins to show signs of putrefaction in four to six days in temperate regions and fewer in hotter ones, unless some degree of embalming is undertaken—and the results of that weren't always satisfactory (see Chapter 3). The Romans didn't normally practice embalming but washed the body constantly in hot water and oil and hoped for the best. But with members of the imperial family, who went on display for a week or more, and high-ranking military officers transported from the provinces (some from as far away as Gaul and Britain), they had no choice. If things went badly, they resorted to a dressed-up wax simulacrum. What can happen when an unembalmed body remains aboveground for a protracted period is demonstrated in the case of Queen Elizabeth I. At her request she was not embalmed. For reasons beyond her control her lead-lined coffin lay in Whitehall for thirty-four days, during which, as one of the watching ladies-in-waiting reported, the body "burst with such a crack that it splitted the wood, lead and cere-cloth; whereupon the next day she was fain to be new trimmed up."

Some cultures don't display their dead, often because disposal is so speedily conducted: Zoroastrians, on the very day of death, unless death occurs near or after sunset; in the religions of the Middle East—Islam, Judaism—preferably within twenty-four hours and no later than within forty-eight. Irrespective of how quickly Jews are buried, their tradition specifically frowns on public viewing of the deceased; even family viewing can't take place after the *tahara* or ritual washing, because the casket is sealed immediately afterward.

 ## The Vigil and Other Customs

Up to the Second World War people in the Western world usually died at home, and the corpse was laid out in bed or in the best (rarely used) front room and friends and relatives were invited to say their good-byes. Now, with the majority of deaths taking place in a hospital or hospice (from whence the dead are delivered directly into the funerary process), viewing has declined, although it remains relatively strong in Catholic countries. In Spain, for instance, viewings are arranged at the city morgue, the *tanatorio*. *Morgue* is a word to chill the imagination, but *tanatorios* are bustling places, rather like small airport terminals, with TV monitors listing cubicles rather than flights (departures, no arrivals), a cash dispenser in the foyer and a bar-cum-restaurant doing brisk trade. There is grief and tears—and respect—but everything is commercially packaged.

Catholic Europe still largely tries to maintain the vigil, with a watcher staying with the corpse every hour of the day and night until the funeral, and it remains a steadfast custom in other world religions. In Ireland the vigil is known as the *wake,* indicating there was originally an element of sensible precaution—the dead actually mightn't have been—though there were darker reasons, too (see Chapter 6).

In many cultures the custom was to put out the fire in the hearth at the moment of death. In a sense this

THE wake was universal in Christendom up to the Reformation. The corpse, with a plate of salt on its breast, was placed under the table, on which something alcoholic for the watchers was provided. The practice gave us the expression "drink you under the table."

THE ghost of Melissa appeared to her husband Periander (dictator of Corinth in the sixth century B.C.) to tell him that she was cold because her garments had been buried instead of burned; the women of Corinth lost their wardrobes to provide her with one via the flames. Just as they send money to the dead, the Chinese send paper clothes—and anything else they think might be useful, from cars to furniture—in the same manner. Coincidentally the ancient Celts used the funeral pyre as a direct postal service to send letters to their ancestors.

was odd, as there was a belief that the soul, turfed out of its now defunct earthly domicile, felt the cold. But a conflicting belief was more important: being in an initial state of confusion, the just-emerged soul might be confused further by the fire, or frightened by it, and might not find its way—which is why in many societies the dying were positioned with their feet toward the door. The ever-complex Chinese were and are among those who don't orient their dead in this way; believing that the soul can depart in different directions, they call upon a diviner, who decides the correct orientation through astrology and *feng shui*.

Another widespread custom immediately after death was to throw out or cover standing water in the house, out of fear that it might "drown" the soul or steal some of its essence (which is why primitive peoples don't want their photo taken). Mirrors were turned to the wall, and even reflective surfaces were covered, for the same reason. By the time this practice was largely abandoned in the early part of the last century—though it still happens in parts of Europe, including Ireland—it was seen only as a rejection of personal vanity. Stopping the house clocks and drawing the curtains also occurs here and there, but no one douses hearth fires, a custom that would be rendered irrelevant now due to central heating.

 ## The Funeral: A Good Send-off

In all cultures the funeral, with its religious and secular trappings, has been the keynote of death, whenever it occurs—often within hours in Zoroastrian tradition, perhaps after months in China, depending on what the diviner calculates is the propitious moment. Muslims like to be buried at night, which is when Muhammad was consigned to the ground. The Romans in the earliest period were buried at night too, in the entirely temporal hope of attracting smaller crowds—funerals frequently turned into fistfights between rival political factions. Later, only children and the poor were buried at night,

IN late eighteenth-century Europe the dead were often driven to the cemetery after dark, though not for burial—they were "parked" until the next day. Many countries had the problem that in the daytime drivers of coffin wagons used to stop off at taverns, then went on their way roaring drunk. Laws were passed making night delivery obligatory. Even if the drivers tippled, at least fewer citizens were around to be shocked by their behavior—or at risk from their road use.

though the flaming torches, which in the darkness lighted the way for the dead as well as the living, were retained. The funeral is so important in Orthodox Judaism that all Jews are commanded to follow any funeral procession that passes, if only for a few paces.

In the West today most who see a passing funeral are indifferent to its significance. The custom of a man removing his hat (baseball cap?) or making the sign of the cross, common until thirty or forty years ago, would be as alien to younger people as the Egyptian ceremony of the Opening of the Mouth and Eyes (which re-animated the mummy, allowing it to see, hear, speak, eat, and drink).

And yet a good send-off is still important. As the Beat poet Allen Ginsberg wrote, when he died he didn't care what happened to his body—just so long as he had a big funeral.

Little old ladies who save their pennies in a bank account to pay for their send-offs expect nothing lavish, but they want the respectable basics—an age-old desire. Many Romans belonged to funeral societies, paying monthly dues so that their cremated remains got a niche in the wall of a columbarium—an inexpensive way to guarantee passage to the afterlife. The Victorian poor put themselves into penury paying for a good send-off, aping the burgeoning middle classes, who aped the aristocracy. *The Times* in 1875 decried "the prodigious funerals, awful hearses drawn by preternatural quadrupeds, clouds of black plumes," as well as ostentatious coffins, as "the vanity of human progress."

A good send-off for any Roman of importance included a funeral oration, for which the funeral procession stopped off at the Forum. Preferably it was given by the deceased's son, in the presence of the deceased, who was stood up to hear it. As the purpose was to inform the deceased how much he'd be missed, the oration was prone to exaggeration, as is the modern eulogy; it's rare indeed that the subject is not a better and more interesting person in death than in life. Roman funeral processions were elaborate affairs, so much so that expenditure on them was finally restricted by law.

WHEN it came to funerals, the ancient Egyptians knew how to push the boat out—as cemeteries were on the west bank of the Nile where the sun symbolically set, the dead went by barge.

The funeral processions of Roman emperors provided magnificent send-offs with the deceased dressed in gold and purple and ending up on a funeral pyre as many as six stories high, with an incense-filled chamber at each level decked out with gold, ivory statues, and paintings. An eagle was released from the top of the pyre to carry the emperor's soul to the gods.

In every age dead heroes have received their nation's greatest respect. Horatio Nelson, killed at Trafalgar, had a funeral car drawn by six horses, and decorated with a carved resemblance of the prow and stern of his flagship. The duke of Wellington, encased in four coffins—pine in lead in English oak in Spanish mahogany—had a funeral car of bronze, the gilded panels of which commemorated his most celebrated military victories.

The viewing of the famous dead could be a dangerous affair: hundreds of people were hurt in the crush in 1926 when Rudolph Valentino was exhibited in a glass-sided casket. At least no one died (if you don't count the several suicides); there were seven deaths and 4,500 injuries during the lying-in-state in 1952 of Eva Perón, wife of the Argentine dictator, when 2 million people passed by her coffin.

EDWARD VII's body was viewed by half a million people in Westminster Hall in 1910; 800,000 saw the body of George V over four days in 1936. Assassinated U.S. president James Garfield drew a crowd of 150,000 in two days in 1881; in 1963 John F. Kennedy attracted 250,000. When Victor Hugo was interred in the Pantheon in 1884, 2 million followed his cortege. Abraham Lincoln holds the record for being physically viewed—more than 7 million Americans saw him as the funeral train traveled slowly from Washington to his burial place in Springfield, Illinois, the coffin opened at each halt.

Musicians led the way, and there were buffoons, actors, and jesters—something the Romans copied from the earlier Etruscans. A family member who looked most like the deceased wore a wax mask of him, as other family members did of ancestors they resembled.

Wherever the buried or cremated remains ended up, the group feasted at the spot. Nine days later they were back again for an even more elaborate revel involving funeral games—including displays of armed combat, the origins of gladiatorial spectacle in the arena—and prodigious amounts of food and drink. Portions of food were set aside for the deceased, and wine was poured into an amphora jug leading directly to the remains (many

FUNERARY flowers are seen as a mark of respect, but they were originally deployed to disguise the corpse's putrefaction. The flowers for Queen Victoria's funeral in 1901 cost over £80,000. In 1997 the sale of flowers in Britain increased by 25% as people paid their respects to Princess Diana after her death in a Paris car crash. The pile of flowers left outside Kensington Gardens was in some places 5ft deep; the bottom layer started to compost at a temperature of up to 180°F.

tombs had lead pipes leading underground for a more permanent arrangement), with provisions left behind to keep the deceased going until the next time. These were usually stolen by the hungry, but no matter. The family returned often enough for many tombs to be equipped with a table, while the really well heeled built a funerary house on the edge of town, complete with kitchen.

Eating and drinking with the dead was common in all ancient cultures, but none perhaps knew how to

THERE'S a banal reason for the snail's pace of a funeral cortege, which has extended to the motorized one. It recalls earlier days when lighted candles were part of the procession, and the pace had to be slow to keep them from going out.

party quite like the Romans. In the Western world, where the English have a reputation for providing post-funeral guests with a small sweet sherry and pallid cucumber sandwiches, only the Irish have a reputation for exuberance. The difference between an Irish wake and an Irish wedding, it's joked, is that at a wake there's one less drunk. It isn't much of a wake if at the end of it some of the guests aren't doing a passable imitation of the main participant.

Yet considering that for a large part of the twentieth century it was known as a land of bachelors, Ireland had no tradition, unlike many other societies, of believing that marriage was an essential ritual of life and to die unmarried was unthinkable. In contemporary Slavic countries the funeral of a single person is simultaneously his or her wedding. In a Romanian wedding-funeral hymn they sing: "Oh, good young man / It was not yet time to die / It was time for you to take a bride / Get up! Look around / There are many friends at our house / Who have come because they thought / We were having a wedding."

The Chinese of Singapore may arrange a wedding between two dead elders so that a younger sibling does not break with tradition and marry first. In Taiwan the living may marry the dead, with a night of (symbolic) consummation, which will allow entry to the ancestral abode.

In 2001 a 71-year-old retired Romanian cobbler named Alexandru Nitu staged a rehearsal for his funeral in the village of Afumati to ensure that the send-off he would eventually receive would go according to plan. "I said to myself," he was reported as saying, "maybe my five children wouldn't do this properly after I am dead." Friends and relatives came to the service as he requested, but it had to be abandoned when mourners would not stop laughing. Still, Nitu was following in famous footsteps. The Holy Roman emperor Charles V spent the last three weeks of his life at a monastery enacting his funeral daily.

Contemporary Mormons who believe that any of their forebears were married other than according to Mormon law can raise them up in a complex ritual to have them remarry and thus enjoy a better place in heaven.

Despite her criticisms of the funeral industry, Jessica Mitford was not against the splashy send-off. The unpretentious funeral, she once said, was for "Unitarians, Quakers, egg-heads and old farts."

 ## Wailing and Other Demonstrations

No Roman funeral would have been complete without public demonstrations of grief and loss. The bereaved wore dull woolen clothing, which they did not change while in mourning, and they remained unwashed and unkempt, as in ancient Egypt where, Herodotus observed, the female relations

> smear their heads with dust and sometimes also the face, and then they leave the corpse in the house and themselves wander through the town and beat their breasts with garments girt up and revealing their breasts. . . . And the males beat their breasts separately there too with their garments girt up.

It was common in most early civilizations to tear (rend, as the Bible has it) your clothing, a practice called *kriah* in Judaism, said to date back to Jacob's reaction to the supposed death of Joseph. Today many Jews display a black ribbon and tear that instead—rather less expensive than ripping a jacket or a dress, which by tradition mustn't be repaired. Dumping refuse over oneself was common in most early civilizations, and the need to be debased in the face of death has modern echoes: for example, the custom in parts of Indonesia for widows to smear their bodies with fluids from their deceased husbands' corpses. Going beyond breast-beating into beating oneself up was also common: in Central Asia mourners still lacerate the arms and face, and in some Aboriginal cultures widows have sometimes taken firebrands to their breasts, arms, and legs so enthusiastically that the single grave has become a double. No wonder ancient Rome finally banned "excessive mourning."

Pretty universally, wailing was *de rigueur* and remains so across the Middle East and in Greece. In China the wailing of a daughter is thought to be particularly beneficial in easing the soul's passage through the many realms of the Chinese underworld. Strictly speaking, Islam believes that wailing questions God's decision to terminate the life contract of the deceased, and sometimes women as the main perpetrators are prohibited from funerals. Wailing enjoyed some popularity during the European Middle Ages—as you might expect, when religious orders flogged the skin from their own backs in the expiation of sin, and priests did the same from the backs of their parishioners—but ardor for it was ultimately lost. Wailing is not unknown in Latin countries but is certainly not practiced in cooler northern Europe: a matter, perhaps, less of religion than of temperament.

 ## Mourning, Noon, and Night

All cultures with elaborate mourning traditions have customs individual to them—such as sleeping on the ground or not wearing leather shoes—but abstention from sex was widely observed and is still a part of the ritual in Judaism and many African societies. It's not an observance among the Nyakyusa tribe of Tanzania, however, where younger men and women copulate at the graveside as a mark of respect. If you've got to go, you might as well go with a bang.

Anthropology suggests three phases to the mourning process. In the first, the relatives of the just-dead are separated, symbolically or in fact and degree, from society, because they are tainted by death. In the second, they adopt specific modes of behavior and dress, which vary across cultures: the Chinese believe it takes three years for the spirit to get where it's going and settle in, for example, while the Iroquois, who once thought the transition took a year, have now cut that to ten days (the speed of modern communications). Finally, after an appropriate cleansing ceremony, often very elaborate, the relatives are readmitted to society.

The living's responsibility to the dead has never ended

ON returning from the burial it is customary for a Jewish family to provide mourners with a meal that includes hard-boiled eggs and bagels—whose roundness symbolizes the continuance and eternity of life.

FOR a year and a day a Victorian widow wore black crepe and a black ribbon sewn onto her underwear. She continued to wear black silk for a second year, after which she was allowed to go into "half mourning"—gray, lavender, or violet in addition to black. For several decades after the end of the Second World War, a widow in Britain wore black for a "respectable" period; now she may not even wear black to the funeral. People wore a black armband to denote loss, something that virtually no one in England does now except soccer players following the death of someone famous or a national tragedy: heart-on-sleeve respect. The British have an increasingly secular society: a tribute to the just-dead is most likely to be a drink at the pub after the funeral. Queen Victoria, the dumpy little widow of Windsor, would have been shocked by it all. She spent forty years in widow's weeds, in mourning for her dear Albert, and for forty years hot water was provided every morning for him to shave, and his clothes laid out, too. Even a culture with the most elaborate mourning procedures might consider that a tad excessive.

here. Keeping their memory alive is important, particularly in societies where ancestors are felt to be closer to the living than in the West, as in Africa and China. In some societies ancestors are believed to become gods. In peasant Russian Christianity ancestor veneration has become muddled up with the veneration of saints.

URBAN MYTH: The Victorians didn't invent the etiquette of mourning—they just made it infinitely more complicated and raised it almost to fetishism. In Restoration England the rich wore black on bereavement and made the sacrifice of it being in wool instead of their customary silk. The rules applied most strictly to men, who wore black buckles and sashes and attached black "weepers"—thin strips of material—to the back of their hats. As shoes also had to be entirely black, there were special ones made of cloth. For his brother's funeral middle-class Samuel Pepys blacked the soles of his everyday shoes and hoped no one would notice in church.

Prayer: A Power Tool

Prayer is crucial—daily in China, Korea, and Japan and among most Aboriginal peoples—and is a two-way street: the living and the dead help those on the opposite side of the divide. In China the soul tablet—which becomes the residence of the deceased once a final dot in vermillion ink or blood is made on it at the gravesite—joins others on the family altar, and they are not only prayed to but contacted simultaneously—like a "send-all" e-mail—to be told about births, weddings, and other family events. Zoroastrians believe that prayer keeps the line to heaven open, and if the connection is broken, it cannot be reestablished.

Prayer was considered vitally important in medieval Europe. Whole monasteries were set up to pray for the dead, and the Catholic Church made it a matter of doctrine that prayer could forgive any sin—for a price. Medieval men and women feared eternal damnation as much as the ancient Egyptians and took every step they could to avoid it. The Church's coffers bulged. Everyone bought "indulgences" to clear their own and dead relatives' sin-debt; many of the poor spent their last pennies on these equivalents of Get Out of Jail Free cards. Those who went off to fight in the pope's Crusades were granted "plenary indulgences," the platinum credit card of indulgences, which forgave sins not yet even committed. The rich hired the poor to do their praying for them, which also involved whipping and torturing themselves to atone for the sins of their wealthy patrons. The rich have always wanted to have their cake and eat it—the ancient Egyptians, Greeks, and Romans even hired professionals to do their public mourning for them. In Greece (where the practice continues) the women of Aaria were much in demand for their impressive wailing.

Wanting to have its cake and eat it too cost the

THERE are other ways of keeping memory of the dead alive. Busts and statues have always commemorated individuals; statues have been called "people in stone." The ancient Egyptians believed that a statue, once animated by the Opening of the Mouth and Eyes ceremony, could be physically present in any number of locations. Today the nomadic Arctic peoples carve a wooden doll and keep it for years, treating it as the person themselves; they set it in a position of honor, make food offerings to it, and take it on family outings; widows sometimes sleep with it in their bed.

Since the beginning of civilization every culture has created wax portraits and taken death masks, in wax, later plaster, and now in other materials, too. In medieval France and England death masks were taken from kings and queens and used on effigies placed on top of the coffin while the corpse lay in state. The earliest known example is of Edward III (1377), which clearly shows evidence of the stroke that killed him. The finest is of Henry VII (1509). France's were all destroyed during the Revolution—but Henri IV (1610) was exhumed nearly 200 years after he died so his impression could be taken.

In addition to death masks, the Victorians, possibly the most death-obsessed people since the ancient Egyptians, filled their houses with portraits and photographs of the deceased and utilized a lock of the dead person's hair in various pieces of jewelry.

Catholic Church dearly. Protestants argued that only God was able to forgive sin. The Church was forced to pull in its horns and concentrate on confession and penance doled out by the parish priest, but the religious unity of western Europe was destroyed, leading to the Reformation. The intensity of religious respect for the dead began a slow decline, which sped up in the nineteenth century with Darwinian rationalism.

The religious perspective of the Renaissance cleric-poet John Donne (who preached his last sermon dressed in the shroud he would soon wear in his coffin) is much fainter, yet these words still have meaning for many:

> *Any man's death diminishes me, because I am involved in Mankind*

Even a cynic would have to admit, if only biologically, that the living are a link between those who have been and those who are yet to come. For better or worse, we're all in this living-and-dying thing together.

HEAVEN, HELL, OR REINCARNATION?

 Dead Boring Underworlds

The many qualities of the ex-Beatle George Harrison were lauded in the tributes to him after his death in November 2001, but it was also observed by some that he was a "miserable git." If this was true, he would have made a good Sumerian.

The Sumerians initially believed that humans were put on earth only to serve the gods by building temples and providing them with food, and that when they died, they were simply extinguished. Later Sumerian thought constructed an underworld, a gray place where the dead were rather like photographic negatives of their former selves. This was the afterlife envisioned in later civilizations, including the Greek *(hades)*, Hebrew *(sheol)*, Hindu *(patala)*, Scandinavian *(hel)*, and Chinese ("yellow springs"). These underworlds did not distinguish between the just and the unjust (although the Greeks had Tartarus for the very few spectacularly evil, like Sisyphus, the mythological king of Corinth, condemned for all time to roll a huge boulder uphill). Except among the ancient Egyptians and Celts, who transferred to their underworlds the best of what was available on earth, in these underworlds the human dead had nothing to do but hang around and be miserable. "Spare me your praise of Death," the great Achilles tells Odysseus on his visit down below. "Put me on earth again, and I would rather be a servant in the house of some landless man, with little enough for himself to live on."

Interestingly, ancient peoples generally believed that a very few "exceptional" dead—pharaohs, kings, heroes, and holy men—got a better deal, a transfer to a paradisical earthly island a great distance over water, a place of endless sun, fresh fruit, and freedom from work—what we might call a package vacation, but which lasted forever instead of for two weeks. The location of this island depended on geography. Mesopotamians thought it lay to the east, in the Indian Ocean; the Chinese thought it lay east too, but in the

Pacific. Ancient Egyptians, Greeks, and the Celtic tribes of Europe placed it in the west, in the Atlantic. Situated between Pacific and Atlantic, the Aztecs had not one island but two, although neither was for the ordinary dead, who shuffled off into the underworld like the ordinary dead everywhere else. In the Middle Ages the Norse Valhalla was only for those slain in battle: here, in a splendid conception of eating, drinking, and fighting, the horrific wounds they inflicted on each other magically healed at the sound of the dinner bell.

As civilizations advanced, their understanding of the hereafter became more complicated. Heaven and hell entered the picture. So did the matter of reincarnation and resurrection and the thorny question of whether or not the dead in some way needed their physical body. For more than three thousand years the ancient Egyp-

BECAUSE the Bible doesn't say the Garden of Eden was destroyed, Hebrew, Christian, and Islamic traditions maintained faith in its continued existence. Medieval Europeans, like ancient peoples, believed in an earthly paradise where the elite dead would go but only until the Last Judgment. It was a belief that lasted until the age of global exploration. Christopher Columbus thought he'd found Eden at the mouth of the Orinoco River in the Atlantic Ocean. Amerigo Vespucci thought it was Brazil.

tians believed that they did. Jews, Christians, and Muslims have never been quite able to shake the idea.

Soul: Food for Thought

For all of history the question has been: What part of us goes onward to the afterlife? Today most in the West believe it's the essence of the individual that survives physical death, the soul, the body dropping away like the spent stage of a space rocket.

This was not the belief of Old Testament Jews and the original Christians, who like the ancient Egyptians considered the human being to be an organic unity: the soul wasn't some homesick visitor from the eternal regions but was inseparable from the body. This is why the Egyptians made such desperate efforts to stop physical decay and why Judaism and Islam still forbid cremation, something that contemporary Christianity has only relatively recently accepted. The idea of resurrection remains strong in popular belief among Christians because of Jesus's supposed arousal from the dead and ascent into heaven. It was not an image that impressed James Joyce's Stephen Hero, who wondered why the Son of God had chosen to go off headfirst, like a rocket, which surely made him dizzy, rather than go by balloon.

Resurrection remains a curious concept, because physical decay, while it can be slowed down, is inexorable. (Did you mention cryogenics? Well yes, see Chapter 3.) Ultimately, as the Bible says, you return to dust and, to paraphrase Hamlet, are likely to be plugging up a keyhole somewhere. When Gabriel (Israfil in Islam) toots his horn and the dead awaken, it'll be a case (to quote another Joycean questioner, Leopold Bloom) of "Every fellow mousing round for his liver and his lights . . . Find damn all of himself that morning."

Does the body become reassembled at the age at which the owner died? Nabokov raised the question in his poem-novel *Pale Fire:* "What moment in the gradual decay / Does resurrection choose? What year? What day? / Who has the stopwatch? Who rewinds the tape? / Are some less lucky, or do all escape?"

Being reunited with the body might be recompense to someone who died young, but would be less attractive to someone who died old and who thus might be decrepit for all eternity. Islam and Zoroastrianism solved the problem neatly. Faithful Muslims are said to arrive in heaven in bodies of perpetual youth, the men beardless but with (lucky) green moustaches. (Sinners, however, rise up deformed according to their sins: the judgmental, blind; the hypocrites with pus running from their mouths; the vain, deaf; and the mute and traitors as pigs.) Zoroastrians say that those who died as adults and enter paradise will be healthy forty-year-olds forever, while those who died young will be permanently youthful. The happy-go-lucky Celts thought that in the afterlife everyone got a new body or the old one was reconditioned as good as new. So did the ancient Egyptians, who preserved their earthly body not for the afterlife but as an important base-cum-vehicle for getting there.

The ancient Greeks conceived of a soul, but as a kind of quasi double of the human individual. In the *Iliad* Homer depicted the soul as having height, eyes, voice, and garments resembling those of the deceased. In Western thought it was Plato who first suggested that the flesh could be separated from its essence, the soul.

Down the ages people have watched the dying,

 IN Nigeria it's believed that the shadow of a person is the shape of their soul. In some cultures people feared to go out of their houses at noon—no shadow, no soul—and on the Malay Peninsula they don't bury a body at noon for the same reason: the mourners' shadows mustn't fall on the grave, because death will follow. Among the Malays and Javanese, food touched by another's shadow won't be eaten because, again, death will follow.

hoping to see the soul make its exit. Renaissance doctors dissected cadavers, trying to locate it without success, despite occasional claims to the contrary—such as at the first autopsy performed in the New World at Santo Domingo, Hispanola, in 1533, which determined that Siamese twins had a soul apiece.

In Western thought we're used to the concept of having a single soul, but it wasn't always so. Early Jews and Christians—like the Egyptians, Indians, Persians, Muslims, later Greeks, and Romans—believed in two souls, or a soul in two parts: the higher, which would make the onward trip, and the lower, which had trouble severing its link with the body. This view is also held by most tribes in Africa, by Lapps, and among Australian Aborigines. At various periods in Chinese thought the individual has been decreed to have between three and ten souls, and Hindu and Buddhist thinkers suggest five—though in ever more complexity, these constantly change form: no single one is the self, but all act on each other, survive death, and finally produce a new physical life.

 ## Reincarnation: Back to the Beginning

Belief in the rebirth of the soul after death into a new physical body for those who deserved it—reincarnation, transmigration, metempsychosis, choose your description—was central to ancient Judaism (once it came into contact with Zoroastrianism during the Hebrews' captivity in Babylon). Today reincarnation for one and all is the cornerstone of most Asian religions and is a matter of faith for some two-thirds of the modern world population. It all depends on karma—the life you've led and that you've just left. It could mean coming back as another human but, just as possibly, as a microbe or a mammal. Indian Jainist monks sweep the street as they walk along so as not to kill any insects— you never know who they might have been. Tibetan Buddhists believe that the original Dalai Lama is reincarnated in each of his successors. When the Dalai Lama dies, his soul immediately occupies the body of a child born at the moment of his death—and a search begins for the soul boy. In Nepal the king is regarded as the reincarnation of the Hindu god Vishnu; the Nepalese also have a living virgin goddess known as Kumari who steps down on reaching puberty, when a new reincarnation is sought.

Throughout history people of various or no religious beliefs have claimed to have lived before. The Greek philosopher Empedocles (490–30 B.C.) said he'd previously been a fish, a bird, a maiden, and a youth (but as he also threw himself into the Mount Etna volcanic

TIBETAN Buddhism has an older reincarnate than the Dalai Lama. The Karmapa is believed to be the repository of an unbroken line going back 2,500 years to the time of Buddha himself. The first Karmapa was recognized 900 years ago—400 years before the Dalai Lama.

The sixteenth Karmapa died in 1981. His letter of prediction was found eight years later, and it took three years to find his 6-year-old successor. In 1999, when he was 14, he fled from Chinese-ruled Tibet and joined the Dalai Lama in India.

crater to prove himself divine, you might want to take that with a pinch of lava). The radical English feminist Annie Besant (1847–1933) remembered being a female martyr in the fourth century and the philosopher Giordano Bruno, being burned at the stake in Rome at the beginning of the seventeenth. A couple of years ago the actress Shirley MacLaine announced that in another life she had had an affair with Olof Palme, the Swedish prime minister assassinated in 1986, and was a lover of Charlemagne before his death in A.D. 814. It's been noted that remembrance of lives past tends to be of the famous or those close to them: a former existence as a foot soldier or chambermaid is considerably less usual. Interest in the possibility of reincarnation has recently revived in the West through "regression"

IN Tibetan Buddhism the soul has numerous adventures before getting reincarnated, including watching men and women on earth making love. When it's attracted to one of the partners, it enters into the lovemaking, sparking conception.

under hypnosis, although this practice appears more likely to convince celebrities and others that they were sexually abused as children than that they've been here before as someone else.

To the Western way of thinking, rebirth, at least in human form, seems a pretty attractive proposition, but that's not what Hindus and Buddhists traditionally strive for. Here on earth each seeks to reject his or her lower instincts and to build up sufficient enlightenment to be worthy of personal extinction—Hindu *moksha,* which allows the soul or divine spark to return to the supreme spirit Brahama; and Buddhist *nirvana,* which allows absorption into collective nothingness. Few have a karma in pristine enough condition, so the cycle of birth and death doesn't stop. For Buddhists this can mean a detour into a variety of hells but also into a variety of heavens that are not exactly like heaven the way the Bible tells it.

The Underworld Gets Upgraded

The Egyptians, Greeks, and Persians were the first to make their empty underworlds into fully ethical systems where saints and sinners got their just deserts, with profound effects on Judaic, Christian, and in turn Islamic thought. The Egyptians divided their underworld into twelve regions or caverns, each corresponding to one hour of the sun god's Superman-like nightly whiz around the globe. As hour succeeded hour, Ra's barque, sailing on the underground river, entered cavern after cavern. As each was illumined, the dead threw off their mummy wrappings and experienced a complete life span in the single hour they were in Ra's presence. The righteous enjoyed the kind of afterlife painted on the walls of Egyptian tombs—an idealized version of life on earth. The wicked were subjected to the kind of treatments that other organized religions found so satisfying, they incorporated them. At the end of the hour Ra sailed on, the great cave doors slammed shut, and the dead climbed back into their coffins and slept until the next night.

The Greeks, for all the philosophical basis of their society, were slow to develop the notion of punishing or rewarding ordinary humans in the afterlife. It took the

Romans to open up Tartarus to all sinners and the paradisiacal island of the Elysian Fields to the virtuous, which they relocated to its own space in Hades, complete, according to Virgil's *Aeneid,* with its own sun and stars. Thereafter, broadly speaking, heaven and hell became separate locations.

Where exactly heaven and hell might be has always exercised human minds. Only in myth and imagination have humans visited such places. Heaven is invariably among the stars, which is where the early ancient Egyptians placed the hereafter, though later they relocated it under the earth (which wasn't necessarily a change of mind—Ra disappeared in the west and went under the world before popping up in the east, so up and down were much the same thing). Jewish thought relocated the heavenly bit of *shoel* to the sky; Christendom and Islam saw no reason to disagree. Until medieval times Christians thought of heaven as being not much more distant than the moon, but by ascertaining that this was rather more than twenty-five miles away, astrology brought a theological rethink, and heaven moved beyond the planets. In Buddhist belief the heavenly regions are far to the east of the material world. Sanpoil Native Americans, who maintain a one-stop land of the dead, position it at the end of the Milky Way.

Inevitably, hell has stayed in the realms of the underworld, beneath the earth's crust. Out of step with East and West in this as in other aspects of belief, Zoroastrians see hell as being between heaven and earth.

Assuming you get to one or other destination, you may be able to be more precise, not that you'll be able to pinpoint it in relation to where you've come from—at the end of time the world will be destroyed. Anyway, you probably won't care, getting on as you will with being celestially happy or being wracked in torment.

Conceiving of only one heaven and one hell as the West does, it's difficult to visualize an afterlife with a multiplicity of them. But the Chinese have six of each, and the Zoroastrians seven. Islam has seven heavens (and possibly an eighth top tier for the particularly blessed), and it once had seven hells, though later thought has made them a single, funnel-shaped abyss, not unlike that conceived by Dante in the Middle Ages, with seven portals leading to seven levels. Buddhism has traditionally had eight hells, but the number has multiplied over time and is complicated by variances in Chinese, Japanese, Tibetan, and Indian thought; in the northern Buddhism of the snowy Himalayas there are eight cold hells as well as eight hot ones. Hinduism (twenty-one heavens) has developed more hells than

THE Egyptian Book of the Dead was never a book as such but a collection of around 200 spells that allowed the soul to avoid the perils of the hereafter. Such spells were once buried only with pharaohs, but when papyrus began to be used for writing, "coffin texts" became available to ordinary people. Such spells included a kind of road map to the labyrinthine underworld, ways of avoiding monsters—and how to silence your heart from testifying against you at your judgment.

The Tibetan Book of the Dead, read out loud to someone as they lie dying, gives the soul guidance to nirvana if possible or to rebirth if not. The novelist Aldous Huxley took mescalin on his deathbed and faded away to such readings. If rebirth is to human life, the book gives tips on how to choose the best womb. If things go badly and a hell is the destination, there are tips for negotiating the best deal with the god of death.

any other culture, perhaps as many as forty-two. (Mind, seven nether regions are occupied by serpents and demons.)

 ## For Heaven's Sake

Developed out of underworlds, the concept of heaven has continued to change over time, reflecting the economic, social, intellectual, and scientific views of an age. The Judaic and early Christian heaven of the Book of Revelation was rather like a synagogue; after Christianity became the official religion of the Roman Empire in the late fourth century, it appeared not unlike imperial Rome, laid out on a grid and filled with elegant buildings and pleasure gardens. In this place the dead (in their bodily sheaths—it's hard to give souls form, much less individuality) went naked as in Eden. By medieval times, when heaven was a walled city of castles and opulent enclosed spaces surrounding God's centralized palace, the dead were regally dressed—all lords and ladies at God's court. Alas, whereas a thousand years earlier the heavenly dead were believed to enjoy conjugal love and procreation, they were now, thanks to the medieval Church's obsession with sexuality, assumed to be in a state of purity beyond concupiscence—the Garden of Eden, with clothes.

Hindus, Muslims, and even many ethereal Buddhists remain enthusiastic about heavenly sex.

Not surprisingly, the concept of heaven in non-Western faiths reflects what the cultures that created them saw as perfection. The ancient Egyptian envisaged heaven (more accurately, the pleasant part of the underworld) as a place of fertile fields, healthy animals, boat-building, and banquets—without the bad teeth (caused by the sand that Egyptian bakers put in bread) and the intestinal worms that plagued everybody. In these heavens rivers sound like musical instruments, waters run hot or cold as you desire, trees produce precious substances, and flowers sprout jewels. Almost no heaven is complete without gates of gold or pearl. In Islam, born among the Bedouin tribes of Arabia, heaven is the "garden of delight," where streams of water, wine, milk, and honey flow, where every person has seventy garments that change color seventy times an hour, and where there are plentiful couches for reclining. Everyone is able to eat a hundred times more than on earth and enjoy it a hundred times more. Intriguingly, armpit and pubic hair, considered uncouth, disappear.

What's different about Hindu heaven and the (usually) six heavens of Buddhism is that, unlike the heavens of Muslims, Christians, and Jews, they are temporary abodes. Hinduism doesn't specify how long the heavenly tenure is, but as in Buddhism, it's for those who haven't collected enough gold stars to deserve obliteration but who have enough to enjoy its delights. Buddhist occupancy can last up to 500 years (each day of which is equal to 100 on earth) in the lowest level, and up to 160,000 years (each day equal to 16,000 on earth) in the highest. Ultimately, however, whether thousands or millions of years have passed, an individual's karma becomes exhausted, and the soul loses its power and beauty and in a pitiful state sinks back down here to face rebirth. In China and Japan many Buddhists have gotten fed up with this aspect of the ever-whirling wheel of life and have begun to believe in a heaven of permanent residence.

Since the Renaissance in the fifteenth and sixteenth centuries, and the later upheavals of the Protestant Reformation and Catholic Counter-Reformation, the view of heaven in Western thought has continued to change. Some Christians and Jews insist on the literalness of heaven, and Muslims are hot on the literal Koranic vision. But a scriptural heaven of golden streets and many mansions has increasingly been seen as metaphor and such artistic depiction of it as symbolism. Heaven now is most usually regarded as a condition, not a place, which is imbued with God's presence—"the full reality of God," in theological parlance.

Christian eschatology once took the view that one of the very best bits of being in heaven would be looking down on non-Christian enemies in hell and enjoying their suffering—a view that was relished in popular belief long after it was tucked under the ecclesiastical carpet. As a Church father expressed it:

What a panorama of spectacle on that day! Which sight shall I turn to first to laugh and applaud? Mighty kings whose ascent to heaven used to be announced publicly groaning now in the depths with Jupiter himself who used to witness that ascent? Governors who persecuted the name of the Lord melting in flames fiercer than those they kindled for brave Christians? Wise philosophers, blushing before their students as they burn together, the followers to whom they taught that the world is no concern of God's, whom they assured that either they had no souls at all or that what souls they had would never return to their former bodies? Poets, trembling not before the judgement seat of Rhadamanthus of Minos, but of Christ—a surprise? Tragic actors bellowing in their own melodramas should be worth hearing! Comedians skipping in the fire will be worth praise! The famous charioteer will toast on his fiery wheel; the athletes will cartwheel not in the gymnasium but in flames.

Heaven's problem has been that, once past the rhetoric, the conception is fuzzy around the edges, something that in the nineteenth century Robert Fellowes tried to explain by saying that the pleasures of heaven

AS the faithful anticipate spending quality time in God's presence, it would be helpful to know what he looks like. In polytheistic religions, where there are many gods, some merely aspects of the supreme being, we have a problem. Among monotheistic religions we still have a problem. God is pure spirit without a body, which is why he's usually described in terms of his omnipotence.

"Everyone wants to know what God looks like," you can read on a religious website. "He is the beauty of the rising sun as the brilliance of His everlasting light dances over the endless seas. He is as high as the tallest mountain and as deep as the deepest sea. He is as gentle as a baby's breath or as mighty as the winds of a hurricane. He contains all the colors of the world. God is as vivid as a blue sky on a sunny day. God is as dark as the darkest red clay. His physique has curves, straight lines and everything in between. He is the earth and all that dwells within it. He is the living water of life from which all life comes."

Yes, but what does God look like?

It's hard in present-day Western culture not to give God a physicality and to see him as a William Blake bodybuilder with a long beard, an image itself derived from Renaissance art in general and Michelangelo's Sistine Chapel in particular.

Could God be a woman? In prehistory goddesses were worshiped, not gods, and there was probably a supreme mother. Scripture, in fact, while mostly using male references, also uses female ones.

God's specific maleness derives somewhat from the view that the female is subject to the male and therefore, ipso facto, God must be a man. Some Christian sects use female or unisex language.

There's a story of a kindergarten teacher watching her class drawing, who asks one little girl what she's doing. "I'm drawing God," the little girl says. The teacher pauses: "But no one knows what God looks like." To which the little girl retorts: "They will when I've finished."

were as beyond our understanding as "a man blind from his birth could be made to understand the precise nature of colour." You can't say John Bunyan's *Pilgrim's Progress* sharpens the picture:

> *There we shall be with seraphims and cherubims, creatures that will dazzle your eyes to look on them. There, also, we shall meet with thousands and thousands that have gone before us to that place; none of them are hurtful, but loving and holy, every one walking in the sight of God, and standing in his presence with acceptance for ever; in a word, there we shall see the elders with their golden crowns; there we shall see the holy virgins with golden harps; there we shall see men that by the world were cut in pieces, burnt in flames,*

> EVERYBODY wants to go to Heaven, but nobody wants to die.
>
> —Albert King and Milton Campbell,
> *Everybody Wants to Go to Heaven,* 1970

*eaten of beast, drowned in the seas, for the love
that they bear to the Lord of the place; all well, and
clothed with immortality as with a garment.*

If we were to think of heaven in terms that define our
age, then we might consider a virtual reality heaven.
That sounds like it might be more fun than sitting
around on fluffy clouds, but we would be using vocabulary to describe what may be outside vocabulary's
ability to describe. Heaven may already be virtual reality. It may be something better.

Is the Hereafter Sexist?

Throughout history the lavish funeral was a man thing;
only the rare and remarkable woman received more
than a modest burial. Keen as they were that women
should hop up onto their deceased husband's pyre,
Viking and Hindu cultures didn't suggest that bereaved
husbands should behave likewise.

Some ancient peoples believed that the afterlife was exclusively a male preserve (in Tonga in the recent past it was only for men of rank), but the major religions make no such distinction. Islam is a qualified exception. A unique feature of Islamic paradise is the virgins, or *houris,* specially created by God to be the playthings of men who have the strength of a hundred—presumably because they need it—and grow more attractive every day. Whether or not Muhammad reinterpreted the angels he saw in pictures of Christian paradise, as has

"IN our country, some scholars suggest that a true believer will be offered as many as seventy women in heaven. Are they correct? Being a married woman, I cannot think of my husband having seventy women around him in heaven. I want him to be mine only. Is this possible? Do I commit a sin by entertaining such thoughts? Being a non-Arabic-speaking woman, I am intrigued by the fact that every time a reward from Allah is mentioned for a particular action, it is suggested that it will be given to a man. What is the reward for women, then? In the translation of the traditions of Al-Bukkari, the writer makes the comment that women can never achieve the grade of men with regard to worship. Is the writer correct? Are men superior to women in Allah's judgment?"

—question posted on the Muslim Q&A site www.ourdialogue.com

been suggested, the *houris'* only desire is to please. Martyrs for Islam—who go directly to paradise—have the services of as many as seventy-two, and as Arabs are presumably boob men, the Koran promises that all are "maidens with swelling bosoms." Their bodies are made entirely of perfume, too, and they're perpetually virgins.

There's no reciprocal arrangement for women.

Religion has traditionally blamed woman for humankind's expulsion from the Garden of Eden and for bringing death into the world. In the second century the Church leader Tertullian wrote: "Woman! You are the gateway of the devil. You persuaded him who the devil dare not attack directly. Because of you the Son of God had to die. You should always go dressed in mourning and rags." In Milton's *Paradise Lost* Sin, twin keeper with Death at the gate of hell, is a woman, or at least "Woman to the waist, and fair / But ending foul in many a scaly fold / Voluminous and vast, a serpent armed / With mortal sting."

Christianity hasn't suggested that more women than men go to hell, but in Islam the Prophet thought that would be the case.

Even in creation stories in Africa, woman gets the blame. Among the Gudi and Darasa tribes, it's said that God wanted to see whether man or the snake was worthy of immortality, so he arranged a race. During it a woman stopped the man and started chatting to him. The snake won—so God made it immortal and man had to die. Among the Ashanti, however, it's thought that death was humankind's punishment because a woman beat up God.

 ## What the Hell!

Hell, to religious thinkers, writers, and ordinary human beings, has always seemed more real than heaven. Hell is about endless fire and brimstone, freezing pits of darkness, sulfur and shrieks, weeping and gnashing of teeth—and the endless repetition of physical torture forever and ever. Pain is infinitely more graphic than pleasure. Anyone who's read Dante will admit that it isn't the radiance of paradise that stays in the memory but the images of the damned being harried around the circles of hell. Here are the sinful of all mankind, among them: the simonites—those sellers of indulgences pardoning sin—plunged head-downward in burning rocks; the violent in a desert of blazing sand under a rain of perpetual fire; the gluttonous, ripped and flayed by Cerberus; and the sowers of discord, continually smitten asunder by a demon with a sword: "No cask stove in by cant or middle ever / So gaped as one I saw there, from the chin / Down to the fart-hole split as by a cleaver / His tripes hang by his heels; the pluck and spleen / Showed with the liver and the sordid sack / That turns to dung the food it swallows in."

Hinduism, Buddhism, and Islam have been no less keen on everlasting torture than Christianity. The Egyptians sent their damned into everlasting fire, an element that the Hebrews added to their underworld. They left the concept vague; Revelation went no further than to say that anyone whose name wasn't found in the book of life at the Last Judgment would be thrown into a lake of fire. Early Christians were so taken with hellfire that they embellished it considerably and took in everlasting physical torment. Islam, if anything, has been even keener on both. Hindu and Buddhist hells have their fiery furnaces but, like their heavens, are stopovers between reincarnations. They're some stopovers, though: hell-days are equivalent to hundreds or thousands of human years, ranging from 500 years in the first hell to 16,000 years in the sixth. In the seventh, internment is half a *kalpa,* the length of time it would take an angel to reduce a rock eighty leagues high to ground level, polishing it once every hundred years with a scarf. In the eighth, internment is a full *kalpa.*

Hellfire is not for Zoroastrians: fire is related to the

sun and is therefore sacred, so the Zoroastrian hell is a cold and lonely place, where the darkness is thick enough to grasp and filled with a foul stench.

Nowadays Judaism, which never extemporized on what hell has in store, has nothing to say on the subject, other than it is where God will punish justly. Christianity no longer regards hell as the worst of life on earth, nor heaven as the best. Hell is no longer a magnified Spanish Inquisition. Punishment, like reward, is a condition. Just as heaven is being in God's presence, hell is its opposite. In popular belief and superstition, ever lagging behind official repositioning, traditional hell still exists for many people, however. Certainly up to the middle of the twentieth century, the half-dozen pages of Father Arnall's hellfire sermon in Joyce's *A Portrait of the Artist as a Young Man* scared the bejasus out of generations of young Catholics.

 ## Is Heaven Elitist?

A man arrives at the heavenly gates and is asked, "Religion?" The man replies, "Muslim." The gatekeeper consults his clipboard and says, "Go to Room 5 but don't make any noise passing Room 1." Another man arrives at the gates. "Religion?" "Zoroastrian." "Go to Room 9 but don't make any noise passing Room 1."

Another man. "Religion?" "Judaism." "Go to Room 4 but don't make any noise passing Room 1." The Jew retorts, "I can understand there being different rooms for different religions, but why must I be quiet passing Room 1?" "Because," replies the gatekeeper, "that's where the Catholics are, and they think they're the only ones here."

The charge of elitism can be laid at many doors, notably that of the early Jews, who thought being the chosen race brought the distinction of heavenly exclusivity. Early Christians, and later ones too, believed the same, including those who went to the Holy Land to fight on the Crusades. Their enemy, the Muslim "infidels," thought the same thing in reverse. According to their holy book, the "infidels" who would never enter paradise were the Christians, the Jews, and the polytheists. Moderate Muslims are uncomfortable with that, as are Jews of a relaxed persuasion whose scriptures, strictly speaking, consign gentiles to the flames. The truth is that fundamentalists in any faith may take an elitist view, as though heaven were a club with entry for members only. Jehovah's Witnesses—four to five million worldwide—lean that way. According to their founder, the Pittsburgh businessman Charles Russell, at the end of the world all will die except Jehovah's Witnesses, who will live with Christ on earth for a thousand years; then

THERE are nineteen major world religions, subdivided into 270 large religious groups and many smaller ones. Christianity accounts for 2,015 million (33% of the world population, but falling); Islam for 1,215 million (20%, growing); Hinduism for 786 million (13%, constant); and Buddhism 362 million (6%, constant). Judaism has 17.5 million— under 3%. Some 825 million people have no religion.

40% of Americans attend church on Sundays compared with only 7% of British. Asked in a poll to choose an "inspirational" figure, only 1% of the British named Jesus; 6% named Britney Spears.

when the dead are raised, the most righteous 144,000— which may include some non–Jehovah's Witnesses— will go to heaven. Everyone else will stay in the earthly paradise—so that's all right, then.

 ## Dead Reckoning: The Judgment of Sin

All major religions consider that the actions of the living, both good and bad, will be judged after death to determine the next move. Just as ancient Egyptians weighed the hearts of the dead against the feather of divine justice (and Ammat, the devourer, swallowed those of souls found wanting, denying them access to the afterlife), so

Buddhists and Zoroastrians expect their thoughts, words, and deeds to be similarly weighed. In Buddhism Yana, the god of death—a fearsome chap with red eyes and an erect phallus—does the business. Zoroastrians know before the weighing whether or not they've drawn a short straw. If they have, they're led to the scales by a beautiful maiden; if not, a hag—which somewhat pre-judges the issue. There is more drama to come. To reach heaven (behesht, which gives us our word "best"), souls must cross a bridge that passes over hell and is as wide as the soul is just. Nine spears wide, and the soul is a win-ner. Unfortunately, for the about-to-be-damned the bridge narrows—to the width of a razor blade for the very wicked—pitching them into the abyss. Other religions are attracted to bridges: Muslims make a similar crossing, and Chinese Taoists are thrown off the bridge of pain into a river that sweeps them to reincarnation.

Muslims believe they will be interviewed in the grave by angels, make a flying visit to heaven to learn their eternal fate based on the angelic feedback, and return to their grave to sleep until the resurrection. This period of time passes like a single night, and Muslims are said to dream; presumably those who know they're hellward-bound have nightmares.

There is some disquiet in Western thought as to

when the soul meets its fate. According to the New Testament, it happens immediately; the Old, like Islam, lets the dead sleep until the final judgment:

> *And I saw a great white throne and Him who sat upon it, from whose presence earth and heaven fled away. . . . And I saw the dead, the great and the small, standing before the throne, and books were opened; and another book was opened, which is the book of life; and the dead were judged from the things which were written in the books, according to their deeds.*
>
> *—Revelation 20:11–12*

One wonders whether heaven's records are still manual, or has data been transferred to newer storage and retrieval systems?

Augustine, the first archbishop of Canterbury in the sixth century, attempted to resolve this now-or-later conundrum. Without any biblical justification, he suggested that by passing through a purging fire—location undetermined—those guilty of venial sins, such as overindulging or laughing too much, would finally be saved: heaven through the tradesman's entrance, so to speak. But it wasn't until around five hundred years later that the Catholic Church developed the idea of purgatory, a doctrine that took it down the slippery slope of selling pardons that led to the Reformation. The "vain opinion" of purgatory was denounced in 1529 by an English Act of Parliament.

Purgatory is still a tenet of Catholicism, as it is of Judaism. Protestant and Eastern Orthodox churches (as well as the independent churches of Eastern Christianity such as the Syrians, Nestorians, and Monophysites) insist it doesn't exist: it's heaven or hell period, no get-out clause. Neither position, of course, resolves the problem of when judgment is made, and the Catholic one raises a question as to the point of the Last Judgment, if individual judgment has already been passed. The Zoroastrian solution has much to recommend it: the good and the bad are assigned when they die, and those not sufficiently one or the other are directed to *hamestega,* "the in-between place," a kind of holding tank, or possibly a sin-bin, where they sit it out until the resurrection.

Scriptural writings have always been keen on defining virtue and even keener on defining sin, on which there is remarkable agreement across the prophetic religions. All denounce idolatry and sorcery, discord, jealousy, fits of rage, murder, lying, selfish ambition, dissensions, envy, drunkenness, greed, adultery, or-gies, immorality, homosexuality, male prostitution, and harlotry—a list by no means complete.

Today we might agree that there are absolutes—murder, let's say—but not signing up for fundamental-ist black and white, we want to ask about degree and mitigating circumstances. An ethical code regulates human behavior, but we have a flexible attitude toward run-of-the-mill sin; one man's sin is another's business opportunity. And we have downgraded much that was apocalyptic. Harlotry? A respectable enough career—and no glass ceiling. Homosexuality? Positively em-braced in some parts of the broad church and a perfectly normal expression of affection, as is oral sex, thought by Saint Thomas Aquinas in the thirteenth cen-tury to be the equivalent of murder. He considered masturbation a bigger sin than adultery, which shows

MEDIEVAL Europe invented the sin-eater, a person who ate beside the corpse at the funeral and in so doing took over their sins, giving the departed an un-blemished record to face divine judgment. It was a liv-ing for sin-eaters, but not much of one. They were considered so contaminated by their sin-load, they were unfit to be part of the community and lived in isolation.

PATIENTS who lose their faith when faced with serious illness are at greater risk of dying. A study in two U.S. hospitals has revealed that those who felt abandoned or punished by God were nearly a third more likely to die within two years than those who maintained their belief.

that the goalposts of sin keep moving. It's all very confusing. Perhaps we're not so far from the ancient Greeks, who regarded what is commonly thought of as sin as merely character defects.

It can't be easy to assess wrongdoing. You wonder about inconsistencies; look at some of the things that happen in court—aren't they even more likely across the ages? And given the mass of evidence gathered on so many by the end of time, might mistakes not be made? Can you call character witnesses? Is there any appeal after conviction? Can someone be certain that if they change their religion, their potential future in the hereafter is updated—that, for instance, a Christian who becomes a Buddhist has their permanent heaven/hell/(possibly) purgatorial possibilities changed to temporary heaven(s)/hell(s)/reincarnation(s)/nirvana possibilities?

💀 Eternity Is a Long, Long Time

Heaven or hell? It's a stark choice, irrespective of the notion of time off for good behavior. The choice is not, as has often been pointed out, remotely equitable. Theoretically, if the passing grade is 50 percent, does the candidate scoring 50½ percent deserve eternal happiness while the candidate scoring 49½ percent deserves eternal misery?

Excepting its purgatorial nod to the few, Catholicism maintains a hard-nosed attitude toward the everlastingness of hell. But some other Christian faith groups now assume that rather more sinners than not will be set free, and many other Christians are personally of that mind, whatever the doctrine of their church might say.

Islam has also softened its line. The Koran itself offers the damned little hope, but later, Islam moved to a belief that the Prophet would intercede for those whose sins did not include denial of Allah; now the general if not the fundamentalist view is that, ultimately, it'll be a temporary punishment. Zoroastrianism shares the view. The dead will return from heaven and hell, to which they've gone at death, rematerializing in their bodies at the spot where they died. So, completing an alliterative trio, will those marking time in *hamestega,* who will now be judged. All of those found in negative equity will be condemned to hell again or for the first time, and their suffering will be greater than before, experienced now as it is by both soul and body. After three days the earth will turn into a torrent of molten metal that will engulf everyone. To the righteous it will feel like warm milk; to the wicked the culmination of their pain. But the slate will be wiped clean, and everyone will enter God's kingdom.

There is magnanimity in this scenario—a magnanimity that drove the Christian speculative theologian Origen nearly two thousand years ago to consider that divine compassion would release the fallen angels and even Satan himself. He was posthumously declared a heretic. If your compassion won't stand for it, then consider the view of such sixteenth- and seventeenth-century thinkers as Descartes, Hobbes, and Locke, who came to believe that hell was not eternal and that after the Last Judgment sinners would be destroyed. "This is so plain in Scripture," wrote Locke, "and is so everywhere inculcated—that the wages of sin is death and the reward of the righteous is everlasting life . . . that one would wonder how the readers could be mistaken."

It's possible to believe that what is called the soul continues for a brief time after death and then fades from existence (the belief of Native American hunting tribes); or that the soul becomes a raincloud, fulfills its function and is then spent (the belief of the Pueblo Indians). It's also quite possible to believe in a full-scale afterlife without a heaven or a hell (sub-Saharan Africa has managed without either).

But in faiths not content with an ungraded community of ancestors, there seem to be three options: to believe that only those of your religious practice will be saved (which might put a penalty point on your license for lack of charity); to believe that, although everyone else should by rights be damned, your god will declare a general amnesty; or to believe that all faiths are variations of one faith and all gods manifestations of one God. The idea that all religions are one has considerable appeal, in support of which the story of the elephant and the four blind men is often told. The first blind man felt the elephant's leg and said it was a pillar; the second its side and said it was a tree; the third its trunk and said it was a snake; the fourth its ear and said it was a fan.

We needn't labor the point.

There is, of course, a fourth belief option, that of unbelief, which in every organized religion means an automatic (after)life sentence for atheists, agnostics, humanists, and those who just don't give a damn. The ancient Roman philosopher Seneca thought that an afterlife was an expression of man's conceit and wrote:

"After death nothing is, and nothing, death." He was contemptuous of everlasting damnation and those who believed in it:

For Hell and the foul fiend that rules
God's everlasting fiery jails
(Devised by rogues, dreaded by fools),
Are senseless stories, idle tales,
Dreams, whimseys, and no more.
            —Troades, *translated by John Wilmot,*
                        Earl of Rochester, 1680

The unbelieving Irish playwright George Bernard Shaw was no more enamored of heaven:

At every one of those concerts in England you will
find rows of weary people who are there, not be-
cause they really like classical music, but be-
cause they think they ought to like it. Well, there
is the same thing in heaven. A number of people
sit there in glory, not because they are happy, but
because they think they owe it to their position.
                        —Man and Superman

Perhaps, when it comes to a choice between heaven, hell, and nothingness, believers and unbelievers in their secret hearts would both really prefer a fifth option, as suggested in this nineteenth-century poem by Heinrich Heine:

> *The heavenly fields of Paradise,*
> *The happy country, don't tempt me:*
> *I'll find no women in the skies*
> *Lovelier than the ones I see.*
>
> *No angel with the finest wings*
> *Could substitute there for my wife,*
> *And sitting on a cloud to sing's*
> *Not my choice for the eternal life.*
>
> *O Lord, I think the best for me's*
> *To leave me in this world, don't you?*
> *But first, heal my infirmities*
> *And see about some money, too.*

WHAT DO YOU DO WITH THE REMAINS?

 Grave Concerns

You can't just leave dead bodies lying about, as our ancestors knew. So what to do with them? Some peoples have eaten their dead—it's been said of cannibals that "their bellies are their cemeteries"—but by and large humankind hasn't found that method palatable.

Burying the dead has been the preferred option for perhaps a quarter of a million years and certainly for the last twenty to seventy-five thousand. The first burials may have been unintentional. Hunters who were wounded or ill were left behind in sealed caves to protect them from ravaging beasts. When they got better, they were supposed to push away the stones; if they didn't get better, then they became interesting archaeological finds. Archaeologists have also suggested that burial in the ground was at first an attempt to renew the deceased by planting them. If so, burial is the earliest known human ritual and played an important part in the development of imagination; and it precedes religious significance.

Such notions have led to a fascinating variety of disposal customs, including serving up the dead as a meal for carnivores and carrion birds. The Masai in East Africa leave the dead in the open for the hyenas. In the Solomon Islands bodies are left on reefs for the sharks. The Biami in New Guinea deposit their dead on open scaffolds, out of reach of wild animals but available to birds of prey—a custom once followed by Mandan Native Americans among others. In Tibet, especially when fuel for more normal cremation is scarce, Buddhists, whose duty it is to help all living creatures,

 IN 1972 survivors of a plane crash in the Andes resorted to cannibalism. The Catholic Church declared that no absolution was necessary because the Uruguayan rugby team had been in extremis and had eaten only those who'd already died.

"WE don't want to interfere in the Parsee religion," Jangoo Gagrat told a meeting of the Disposal of the Dead with Dignity Action Group in Bombay, "but Parsees have to face facts. The population of the Indian vulture has declined drastically over the past few decades and nowadays the Towers of Silence are full of decaying corpses, most of them barely eaten. And that clearly constitutes a major public health hazard."

But speaking on behalf of Bombay's fifty-five thousand Parsees, high priest Dastur Nadershah Unvalla refused to consider other forms of disposal. "The scriptures say it is a heinous sin to bury or cremate the dead. Ever since the eighth century we have been disposing of our dead by placing them atop one of our Towers of Silence and letting the vultures strip the bones bare. It's true that Parsees in Europe and America bury their dead, but that is a disgrace and I look down on them."

However, Gagrat's action group is agitating for a change in Indian law. "The government seems unaware that the city's biggest collection of biomedical waste comes from these towers, because eventually even the Parsee priests cannot stand the stench of rotting flesh, and ask the authorities to take away the putrefying remains in specially blessed plastic wheely-bins. Other religions have had to modify their ancient funeral rites in response to urbanisation. Hindus, for example, are often prosecuted for throwing half-burnt corpses into the river. At present, the Parsees are legally

> exempt, but they really have to make a decision soon. Either accept some form of cremation, or else start breeding vultures."
> —*Borneo Bulletin*, 8/12/01

"joint" a corpse and leave it in the high mountains for wild animals—the misleadingly termed "sky burial." A few days later they collect the bones, grind them to powder to mix with flour, and bake bread as a second helping. Since to Iranian and Parsee Zoroastrians earth and fire are elements too sacred to be contaminated by death, and therefore burial or cremation are out of the question, they leave their dead on top of stone "Towers of Silence," to be picked clean by vultures. Built when possible in isolated spots, the towers, which have elaborate drains and charcoal filters to purify the rainwater and a central lime pit for the bones, are abandoned after a hundred years as being too polluted for further use.

 The Physiology of Death

The dead have to be dealt with, not just because they clutter the place up and are poor conversationalists, but because they're a health hazard.

Death, that hath sucked the honey of thy breath,
Hath had no power yet upon thy beauty.

Romeo could say this to the just-dead Juliet, but as little as half a day later he might be lost for words. Everyone knows that the face of death becomes unpleasant, but in an age shielded from death, most don't realize how quickly it can happen. Anyone of a squeamish disposition might like to skim the following description of the physiology of death, or skip it altogether.

When a body dies, it does so bit by bit. No longer being pumped and oxygenated, the blood settles on the underside, making the skin there reddish purple. This is known as hypostasis or postmortem lividity, a condition at its most prominent about ten hours after death. In areas where the body's weight rests, the blood is squeezed out, leaving the skin gray. Muscles contract (rigor mortis), beginning within about four hours: first the eyelids, then the jaw, neck, and shoulders, then other muscles. After thirty-six to forty-eight hours, as the muscle fibers continue to degenerate, the body relaxes but it is now cold.

Meanwhile the millions of bacteria in the gut eat through the lining of the digestive system and then invade the rest of the body. At the same time the blood's hemoglobin turns to sludge. The first sign of decay is usually a greenish patch of blood vessels on the lower belly.

The body also undergoes its own breakdown (autolysis) caused by enzymes and other chemicals released from dead tissue. The pancreas, source of the digestive enzymes, digests itself. Putrefaction spreads as the bacteria proliferate; the veins become outlined on thighs and shoulders. Within a week the body looks "marbled"; the skin has sagged and slipped and developed blisters. The disagreeable smell of hydrogen sulfide and methane has become apparent. Stomach contents may already have been regurgitated into the mouth and air passages. The front of the body starts to swell, making the eyes bulge and the tongue protrude and pushing bloodstained fluids from the orifices. The color of the skin changes to olive to purple to black. The skin of the hands begins to slough off. Within a few weeks the teeth and nails begin to loosen. Within a month or so tissues liquefy, and the main body cavities burst open.

Long before humans can smell decay, the carrion flies have arrived. The first and most numerous are bluebottles or blowflies, which lay eggs on the body—

a single bluebottle lays two thousand eggs. Then come the flesh-fly greenbottles, which are viviparous and lay already-hatched larvae that can start feeding right away. In the tropics a body above ground can be a writhing mass of maggots within twenty-four hours; even in a temperate climate maggots can strip a body to the bone in weeks—they've been called "the unseen undertakers of the world." In *Being Dead,* his novel about a middle-aged husband and wife murdered on a beach and left to rot, Jim Crace describes the flies "lined up like fishermen along the banks of the bodies' open wounds." Other creatures line up for this self-service too, including beetles, gulls, and crabs, which frisk the bodies with the same dispassion "as cows might pay a turnip head."

In a coffin, protected perhaps for years from outside agencies, destruction and putrefaction are much less rapid. The skin shrinks, cracks, and flakes like old paint, but if the corpse remains dry, full skeletonization may take a decade or more. But every "body" is different. Fat people decompose more quickly than thin; those with a fever at death more quickly than would otherwise be the case. A rule of thumb is that one week in air equals two weeks in water equals eight weeks in the ground.

Burials and Bones

Generally speaking, those who are buried (inhumed) go into the ground or into a specially constructed tomb above or below it. But others end up in more curious resting places. New Caledonians and inland mountain people of Borneo are placed erect within the trunks of trees, the bark replaced over them. The Berawan of Borneo are potted in large earthenware jars that are usually used to make rice wine, and after the bodily fluids are drained off, they are interred in smaller receptacles. The Jivaro of South America bury women and children under the floor—just as the first city dwellers did with all their dead in Mesopotamia ten thousand years ago.

Most cultures consider a single burial sufficient, but some also practice a second—a practice that stems

 WHEN an Australian Bushman died, his body was lowered into a grave where a special gravedigger waited to take slices from the corpse to hand to the mourners. A man could eat his sister's husband and his brother's wife but not his children. Children could not eat their father. A mother ate from her children, and children from their mother.

from the atavistic belief that the flesh is corrupt in a religious as well as a physical sense and that the true essence of the deceased resides in the bones.

The belief is as old as humankind, although the earliest evidence of it, from the Stone Age, was interpreted in the early twentieth century as cannibalism or ritual sacrifice. More recent analysis concludes that the bones in Neolithic tombs were disarticulated because they were carefully arranged there once the flesh had disintegrated in burial elsewhere. Not all peoples who practice scaffold burial allow their dead to be eaten by wildlife: in Malaysia, Indonesia, and the Pacific Islands the dead are protected against predators. After a year or more the remains are brought down, and the bones ritually buried. Throughout history in many cultures bones have been polished, sometimes painted or stained—red ochre among primitive peoples—possibly in the hope of bringing the dead back to life. In sub-Saharan Africa, particularly among the Bantu-speaking peoples, the bones of the dead are ground to powder and mixed with ritual beverages. Orthodox Jews and modern Greeks disinter the remains of their deceased three to seven years after primary burial, wash the bones, sometimes in wine, and place them in a columbarium. The second "burial" has greater significance than the first.

Hang-ups About Cremation

Cremation gradually replaced burial in prehistoric Europe toward the end of the Bronze Age. It was the commonest form of disposal in Babylon and Phoenicia and other parts of the Near East, as it now is among Hindus, Buddhists, and many Australian Aborigines. At various times the practice went in and out of favor in the Greco-Roman world as it has in the Judeo-Christian one.

Today Judaism forbids cremation because it seems to interfere with God's right of disposal; Jews must not only be buried—and not in a vault or mausoleum unless it is underground—but if they die in an accident or through violence, even their bloody clothes must be buried with them. Yet the ancient Israelites cremated

 IN contrast to the common view, in India the bones of the dead are considered not only corrupt but dangerous—which is why those collecting them for burial after cremation do so with eyes closed and with liberal use of purifying water and milk. They're then washed again before ritual burial in an urn. In northern India, where cremations are performed on platforms on the Ganges or other rivers, the urn is simply allowed to float away.

heroes and turned to cremation when it was a matter of expediency: the bodies of Saul and his sons, for example, were taken from the wall of Beth-shan and burned at Jabesh to prevent worse indignities at the hands of the Philistines.

Apart from in Germany and Scandinavia, the tradition of burning the dead rather came to a halt once Constantine made Christianity the official religion of Rome in the fourth century and the doctrine of resurrection spread through the empire. Until then the Romans had occasionally delighted in burning Christians and throwing their remains in a river or the sea. Oddly, for a time in the second and third centuries, Christianity seemed happy with cremation, but the strengthening belief that it invalidated resurrection made it forbidden. In the Middle Ages Christians were positively frightened by the prospect of cremation—they associated it with hellfire, and a fiery end was meted out only to witches and heretics.

Until the late nineteenth century, when rationalists concluded that cremation was hygienic, cheaper than burial, and didn't tie up valuable land, the practice was illegal in much of Europe and denounced as a mortal sin by the Roman branch of Catholicism, which didn't sanction it until 1964 (and the Eastern Orthodox Christian churches still haven't). Many Catholics still think cremation is wrong, perhaps, in Leopold Bloom's words, seeing it as "devilling for the opposition."

Cremation was talked about during the French Revolution in a wave of anticlericalism, but the modern method of carrying it out in a closed chamber was pioneered in northern Italy. Secularists and radicals in Britain were in favor, as were many who had observed the Hindu practice in India, for better reasons than those of the seventeenth-century English physician Sir Thomas Browne, who suggested that "to have our skulls made drinking Bowls, and our bones turned into Pipes, to delight and Sport our enemies, are Tragical abominations escaped in burning Burials." George Bernard Shaw was on the barricades. "Dead bodies can be cremated," he said. "All of them ought to be; for earth burial, a horrible practice, will some day be prohibited by law, not only because it is hideously unaesthetic, but because the dead would crowd the living off the earth if it could be carried out to its end of preserving our bodies for their resurrection on an imaginary day of judgement." The clergy were aghast, associating cremation with godlessness. The bishop of Lincoln said it was a heathen practice. The medical profession put forward the not-unreasonable argument that if any skulduggery were involved in a death, then the evidence would be gone in a puff of smoke.

But public opinion everywhere from Germany to the United States was attracted to the idea—paradoxically, the sheer size of the new cemeteries that at long last had replaced the overcrowded medieval churchyards had raised revulsion in many people who were worried that so many bodies in one place would contaminate the air, the soil, and the drinking water. People preferred the idea of elimination in a short, sharp blaze to some of the other ideas of the reformers, the most practical of which proposed either returning to the medieval fashion of burial without coffins—direct contact with the earth ensuring quick decay—or embedding bodies in charcoal in well-ventilated buildings; either method would allow the bones to be gathered up after an appropriate period and stored. Other schemes included

FROM the Napoleonic battlefields of Austerlitz, Leipzig, and Waterloo, hundreds of tons of bones of the fallen, "hero and horse alike," were shipped in 1822 to Yorkshire to make fertilizers. After the Russian-Turkish War (1877–78), 30,000 skeletons amounting to 30 tons landed at Bristol for similar use. The idea of processing human corpses for the common good was frequently suggested by reformers in the nineteenth century and has arisen from time to time since.

using bodies as fertilizer, mixing them with water, and treating them as sewage, or even rendering them down on something equivalent to the Zoroastrian Towers of Silence.

Despite the formation in 1874 of the Cremation Society of England by Queen Victoria's own surgeon (the Cremation Association of America didn't follow until 1913), legal opposition remained; but supporters of the early crematorium movement in England were prepared to flout the law and risk imprisonment. For a number of years the politicians kept out of it, but two celebrated cases finally gave them no option. First, Sir Charles Wentworth Dilke transported his wife, who'd died in childbirth, to Dresden for cremation. Then in 1883 an eccentric Welsh doctor, William Price, who'd cremated the body of the baby son he'd had with his housekeeper (and named Jesus), was tried and acquitted; the judge said cremation was not an offense. There was nothing for it but to make cremation legal.

For several years there was the odd demonstration at crematoria in every country, and police protection was needed. Today, when 70 percent of the British and nearly a third of Americans choose cremation, it's hard to think it was ever such a heated issue. In an age that's even more aware of the environmental impact of burial, it's good to know that, as far back as 1973, a report cal-

SINCE 1988 60,000 graves have been excavated at Shenhu, eastern China, reclaiming land for farming; the bodies are cremated and stored in a 7-story crypt. São Paulo in Brazil and Genoa in Italy have similar structures 10 stories high.

culated that ninety years of crematorial practice had saved Britain an area equal to six hundred soccer fields.

Believing as they do that the transmigration of souls makes the individual body of no account, Hindus and Buddhists have never had a hang-up about cremation—only young children and yogis, who are considered too pure to need the purification of fire, are buried. In contrast to Zoroastrian belief, the fire itself is considered impure and the embers of the pyre are taken at sunrise to a crossroads (see Chapter 6) to be put out.

Burning a body in the ordinary way isn't easy—look at the botched attempts over the years to cover up murder and other crimes. It has to be said that the outdoor cremations in non-Western cultures are frequently less than total. The temperature in modern crematoria receptacles reaches between 1600–1800°F, and even in this constant heat the combustion of an average adult takes two hours. (A rather heavier than average three-hundred-pound male partially destroyed the crematorium at the Meadowlawn Memorial Park in San Antonio, Texas, because his excess fat sent the needle off the clock.)

Most prosthetics, such as hip replacements, aren't a problem, but pacemakers are and have to be removed—they've been known to explode. Crematoria staff dislike breast implants—the gloopy residue is hard to clean up. After a cremation, once the furnace cools down, a powerful magnet removes any pieces of metal. The remains are then run through a processor, and end up as four to eight pounds of what looks like crushed seashells.

An alternative method of disposal that has been experimented with in the United States involves solidifying a corpse in liquid nitrogen, pulverizing it, and then further reducing it by freeze-drying—just like instant coffee.

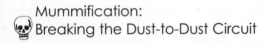

Mummification: Breaking the Dust-to-Dust Circuit

Mummification: embalming. Is there a difference? The words are mostly interchangeable, but where mummification can be accidental, embalming is intentional. Both deprive bacteria of air or water, which kills them off and thus arrests decay. (Stillborn babies hidden by their mothers often mummify because bacteria haven't yet developed.)

Bodies have been accidentally dried out by extreme heat and extreme cold. The hot sands of China's Taklimakan Desert have given up the mummies of a tall, blond Indo-European race that settled the region centuries before the Han Chinese arrived. At the other extreme, a melting Italian glacier has given up a five-thousand-year-old man, and in the icy peaks of the Andes twenty or so Inca children sacrificed five centuries ago were so perfectly preserved that blood was still in their veins. Other bodies have resisted decay in oxygen-depleted peat bogs in England and Denmark. Alternatively a conducive combination of dry soil and

AN overweight body in a certain combination of temperature, humidity, and water can be mummified by *adipocere*—turned into what undertakers call "grave wax" but which to most people looks like soap. The Soap Lady on display in the Mutter Medical Museum in Philadelphia was found when bodies were being moved from an old graveyard more than a hundred years ago. For years the "soap" body of William von Ellenbogen, a soldier killed in the American Revolution, was on display in the Smithsonian Institution.

WAS Jesus embalmed? This from the gospel of St. John: "And there came also Nicodemus, which at the first came to Jesus by night, and brought a mixture of myrrh and aloes, about an hundred pound weight.

"Then took they the body of Jesus and wound it in linen clothes with the spices."

The practice of embalming lingered in ancient Palestine for more than a millennium. As some commentators have pointed out, the Egyptian embalmers used myrrh and aloe as antibacterial agents. If myrrh and aloe were required only for their aromatic smell, a hundredweight seems excessive.

climate can do the job, as occurred in the cemetery in Guanajuato, northwest of Mexico City, where over a sixty-year period a hundred or so corpses were evicted from their plots when their relatives failed to keep paying a grave tax. The corpses became exhibits in a museum that's known around the world.

Assyrians and Scythians preserved their dead in honey, the Persians in wax. (The Macedonian Alexander the Great was embalmed in both.) The ancient Hebrews used spices and aloes. Among the Jivaro of Ecuador and Peru, and in Indonesia, deceased leaders were slowly smoked over a fire for several months, then hung from the eaves of their houses to keep a benevolent eye on life below. In Asia Buddhists still save the bodies of beloved monks by coating them in resin and sawdust, while in Tibet they pack them in salt. Alcohol was widely the most popular preservative for thousands of years. Admiral Nelson came back from Trafalgar in a keg of brandy, his presence in it not dissuading the crew from drinking it—giving rise to the naval expression, "tapping the admiral."

Egyptian mummifiers, though the best known, were neither the first nor the best at the job. The Chinchorro in Chile were mummifying their dead two thousand years before the Egyptians. The Chinese started a thousand years after the Egyptians, but no handiwork carried out on the banks of the Nile approached the standard of some Chinese specimens—for example, Lady Ch'eng, wife of the governor of Huan Province, who was excavated from her tomb in 1972 some twenty centuries after being put in it; her limbs were still flexible, and her skin soft to the touch.

Ancient hunters knew that gutting the animals they caught or drying and salting fish prolonged the freshness of kill or catch. Most embalming depended on these techniques. The Egyptians eviscerated their dead, placing liver, lungs, intestines, and stomach in special urns called canopic jars that went into the tomb. The heart—thought to be the location of intellect and memory—was left in place, while the brain, which the Egyptians didn't see the point of, was thrown away, once they'd withdrawn it from behind the eye or through the nostrils. The cavities were then washed out with palm wine and spices and stuffed with small linen bags of natron, a compound of sodium salts found on several lake shores. Once covered with more natron, the body was left for about forty days to dehydrate, after which it was given a final spell in the sun. In the meantime the family gathered enough linen for the embalmers to tear into strips for wrapping the body—layer upon layer, coated in resin, about twelve hundred yards in all. *Mummy* comes from *mummia,* Persian for bitumen, which was once used in the process.

This was the custom service and could take up to a year. According to Herodotus, who visited Egypt in about 450 B.C., the middle class got the exterior natron and an injection of cedar oil up the anus, which after a prescribed period was allowed to escape, bringing the

EGYPTIANS sometimes kept a mummified body aboveground for several years, using it as security to borrow money. Few people reneged on the deal. If they did, they were refused a burial of their own and forfeited entry to the afterlife.

internal organs, in theory at least, with it. The poor got an abdominal purge and were sent smartly on their way into the hereafter.

Popular belief has it that Egyptian mummification was an art, but only during a middle period was it sophisticated; on the whole it was pretty crude stuff. The embalmers' tents were hardly sterile environments: considerable numbers of beetles and larval skins, and a few small rodents, have been found when mummies have been unwrapped. In 1994 Dr. Bob Brier, a professor at Long Island University, New York, caused a stir

THE lives of the Egyptians were influenced by a variety of animals to an unprecedented degree—and the numbers they mummified far exceeded humans. The most sacred animal was the bull, thought to be divine—there was a cemetery for the mothers of temple bulls.

Chinese emperors maintained a dog cemetery in Peking, with tombstones of marble, ivory, silver, and gold. The Victorians had many pet cemeteries, and today pet cemeteries can be found across the world, from Russia to the Virgin Islands. There appears to be only one pet cemetery-cum-crematorium in Britain. America has 469, the largest being Bubbling Well Pet Memorial Park in Napa, California. Pet cremation is becoming more and more popular—and the company Summum has revived the practice of pet mummification.

by creating a modern mummy using ancient Egyptian tools and procedures. The interesting point is that the experiment showed that the "old leather" look common to the Egyptian dead is a result of the mummification process, not the passage of time.

Embalming spread from Africa and Asia to Europe from about A.D. 500. During the Middle Ages it included removal of the viscera, immersion in alcohol, and the insertion of herbs into incisions made in the fleshy parts of the body, but it was so expensive that even most royals couldn't afford it. Canute is the first king of England known to have undergone the process; Henry I ordered Edward the Confessor's coffin opened to see what embalming had done for him a century and a half earlier before agreeing to it for himself. How well these procedures were conducted is open to debate, but William the Conqueror's earlier embalming in 1087 was a disaster. His corpulent person swelled out of the coffin during the funeral service; two soldiers stood on him to squeeze him back in and broke his spine, which punctured his stomach, causing it to explode with a loud bang and a stench that drove the assembly from the cathedral. In the seventeenth century the attempt to embalm Oliver Cromwell was such a fiasco that he started to reek and was promptly buried.

More recent embalming has sometimes fared no better. King George IV was so badly embalmed in 1830 that his body swelled in his coffin and holes had to be drilled to let out the foul air. In 1927, when George V's wife, Mary, attended the funeral of her brother Adolphus, his body exploded during the funeral procession. When Robert Kennedy saw the poor job of embalming that Dallas morticians had done on his assassinated brother John in 1963, he decided against an open casket viewing.

 ## Miracle Busting

In Russia, where Orthodoxy practices secondary burial, and in other cultures, bodies are disinterred as a matter of course, but medieval Europe seemed to be forever digging people up just to have a look. A hundred or so were discovered to be so well preserved that the Catholic Church declared miracles had occurred.

Many wondered why some of the bodies of Incorruptibles, as they became known, began to rot once they'd been removed from their vaults, but by and large such worries weren't made public. The Incorruptibles, over half of them in Italy, officially became saints or *beati* (the blessed not yet canonized). Since the eighteenth century people have been less credulous. In the last fifteen years a number of the Incorruptibles and their resting places have been examined scientifically, and the preservation of some has been explained by a combination of airtight lead coffins, cool, dry spots under altars unfavorable to bacterial growth, and surrounding alkaline stone. Others, like Saint Beata Christina of Spoleto, were found to have been embalmed by their followers, and one, Saint Clare, founder of the Franciscan nuns, was a fake—a dummy with a mask, although her bones were inside.

The Catholic Church requires two authenticated miracles before it considers a candidate for canonization, and for centuries physical preservation counted as one. That's no longer so, but preservation can be ecclesiastically useful. In 1984, after the death in Rome of the ex-

 IN medieval Europe and Arabia mummy dust was seen as a miracle cure for everything from abscesses to fractures, poisoning to incontinence, paralysis to disorders of the liver. Mummy dust was the "magic bullet" of the day; the French king Francis I wore a small packet of it around his neck for emergencies. Although Egyptologists estimate that the ancient Egyptians mummified more than seven hundred million bodies in their history, medieval Europe was not awash with mummies. But demand was so great that entrepreneurs raided graveyards to meet it. Unbelievably, mummy dust was still being advertised in England at the beginning of the twentieth century.

iled dissident Ukrainian cardinal Josef Slipyj, the Church wanted to make a point about his stand against Communism, so it had him embalmed and returned to Lvov. Two million people lined up to see him in the cathedral before he was buried. The Church didn't say Slipyj looked good for miraculous reasons. What Ukrainians thought was up to them.

 ## Early Modern Pickling

Interest in anatomy during the Renaissance stimulated experiment in embalming methods. Leonardo da Vinci, who dissected at least fifty cadavers, used venous injection to keep them fresh; one seventeenth-century Florentine physician turned a corpse to stone by injecting the tissues with silicate of potash and then immersing the body in a mild acid. While there were charlatans in every age to claim improved pickling methods of their own invention, the Scottish anatomist William Hunter is credited with being the first to report fully on arterial embalming the following century.

Yet it was his younger brother John who made embalming into a trade and a fashion. In 1775 Martin Van Butchell, a quack doctor and dentist, got him to embalm his wife. Her marriage settlement had stipulated that her husband should control her fortune "as long as she remained above ground," and he ensured that's where she stayed. "The Preserved Lady" was such a talking point that strangers dropped in to see her, replete in her finery in a glass case in Van Butchell's drawing room, and he was obliged to place a newspaper advertisement limiting her visiting hours to "any day between Nine and One, Sundays excepted." A few years later, when Van Butchell remarried, his second wife objected to The Preserved Lady's presence, so she was sent to the museum at the Royal College of Surgeons where she stayed until she was "cremated"— in 1941 the college was destroyed in the London blitz.

Demand for embalming grew in the second half of the nineteenth century. In the United States, a new type of undertaker-businessman promoted its advantages

THE English reformer Jeremy Bentham thought burial wasted valuable land and that every man, properly embalmed, could become his own commemorative statue—which he called an "auto-icon." When he died in 1832, Bentham was publicly dissected. His skeleton was wired together, dressed in his clothes, and placed in a glass cabinet. The embalmed head was not a success, and another had to be made in wax. Bentham's effigy sits to this day in its cabinet in the senior common room of University College, London, his own head in a box at his feet.

IN 1891 a French surgeon called Varlot electroplated the dead by making the body conductive by exposing it to silver nitrate, then immersing it in a galvanic bath of copper sulfate, producing a "brilliant red copper finish of exceptional strength and durability." It didn't catch on.

over the customary method of preserving bodies for viewing or transportation—packed in ice or laid on "cooling boards" that had a concave, ice-filled box fitted over the torso and head. Some of these entrepreneurs even exhibited "samples" in their shop windows or toured rural areas with them. The American Civil War—or rather the astuteness of Thomas Holmes, a former New York coroner's assistant who'd been commissioned in the Union Army medical corps—broke down remaining public resistance. Having experimented with preservative concoctions in his previous occupation, Holmes embalmed a few soldiers killed in battle to send home to their families, charging them $100. Abraham Lincoln, in an act of compassion, sanctioned the treatment for all the fallen, and in four years Holmes embalmed 4,028 men. He returned to Brooklyn a rich man. According to his wishes, Lincoln was embalmed after his assassination—and America took to the procedure as though it were a patriotic duty.

💀 The World's Most Famous Embalmees

Embalming came widely into vogue in the "New Age" 1920s, when the discovery of Tutankhamen's tomb sparked interest in all things Egyptian. It prompted the Italians to embalm Caruso, the world's greatest tenor, who lay in state for eight years before he was buried. It also influenced the Kremlin in preserving Lenin. His internal organs were removed, and his body was dunked in formaldehyde to stop tissue breakdown and glycerine for elasticity. Communism's revolutionary leader has been in his Moscow mausoleum (except for a short break to Siberia during the Nazi advance in the Second World War) for almost eighty years. He looks the picture of health, thanks to a formaldehyde bath every eighteen months and a twice-a-week touch-up of the bits that show, but he's not the man he was. Beneath one of his several dozen identical blue acrylic three-piece suits, he wears a wetsuit to keep him from falling apart. In fact, Lenin is now 60 percent wax and his ears aren't his own. But having dispensed with God, Communism needed Lenin as some kind of substitute, and now, despite calls that he should be laid to rest, he's become too much of a national symbol. The embalmed Stalin briefly joined Lenin in his mausoleum until he was posthumously disgraced and banished to the Kremlin wall.

The Soviet Union seemed to think that all Communist leaders, once fallen off their perches, should be physically preserved, and saw to it that the leaders of various Eastern European states and the likes of Chairman Mao, Kim Il Sung of North Korea, and Ho Chi Minh of North Vietnam got the treatment. Mao is now shrinking at a rate of 5 percent a year; a trick of the light, the authorities once said, until the shrinkage became too obvious.

Since the collapse of Communism the former Soviet embalmers have gone private and now make their money by embalming Russian mafiosi.

Lenin is the world's most famous embalmee. Unquestionably Eva Perón, wife of the Argentinian dictator Juan, is the most beautiful, at last sighting. When she died in 1952, her body, in probably the most meticulous embalming ever carried out, was immersed in acetate and nitrate and then slowly injected with wax. The process not only kept her organs intact but made her skin translucent. When hubby was ousted and fled to

UNTIL the discovery of formaldehyde by a German chemist in the late nineteenth century, arsenic was the chief modern embalming chemical. Its use was banned in the early years of the twentieth century.

Paraguay, he left Eva behind. The new regime cut off her left ear and a fingertip (allegedly to check how much of her was wax, but probably as souvenirs). Friends snatched her back, and she traveled the world, including a stop in Rome under the protection of the Vatican. For years not even Perón knew Eva's whereabouts, but in 1971 she was found in a cemetery in Milan, dug up in perfect condition, and delivered to him in Madrid. She's now buried in the family vault under twenty-three feet of concrete.

There are no challengers for Ferdinand Marcos's title as the world's most buffoonish cadaver. His widow, Imelda—whose shoe collection shows she can't throw anything away—had the onetime Philippine dictator embalmed after he expired in exile in Hawaii and famously gave him parties on his birthdays and their wedding anniversaries. On returning to Manila in 1992 she demanded a hero's burial for him, was denied, and so put him on display in an air-conditioned mausoleum, with tasteful music, at his ancestral home. At one point the local electricity company cut off the supply for nonpayment of bills. Ferdy still lies there, seemingly unconcerned.

Whatever such full-scale preservations cost, it's unlikely that many could afford one, but since 1975 a company called Summum in Salt Lake City, Utah, has

IN 1978 Dr. Gunther von Hagens, a German anatomist and self-confessed "modern Frankenstein," developed plastination, to create medical specimens for anatomy classes. The process replaces the water and liquids in the body's cells with polymers—in effect turning them into plastic. It can take 1,500 hours. In 1997 an exhibition of more than 200 plastinated corpses in Mannheim, Germany, provoked a storm of protest and a packed house. Von Hagens' *Body Works* exhibition of 20 whole corpses and 200 body parts—which arrived in London in March 2002—has been seen by 8 million people in four countries so far. "My bodies are incredibly popular," von Hagens says. "Women in particular like to look at the displays. Perhaps they have more body awareness because of childbirth and so on." A Web poll found that two-thirds of respondents were in favor of the exhibition; only 16% found it morally reprehensible.

been offering a method of mummification that updates the Egyptians' and just might be within your means. For around $20,000, not including memorial or funeral service, transportation, or mausoleum storage, Summum will cleanse and replace your organs, immerse you in an aqueous chemical compound that will replace the water in your body and prevent you from drying out, wrap you in layers of cotton gauze, polyurethane, and fiberglass, and completely seal you into a bronze or stainless steel body-shaped Mummiform—with Egyptian motif another $36,000—using amber resin.

To date, one hundred forty-seven people are claimed to have made arrangements to be mummified, but Summum still awaits its first client.

 ## Cryonics: A Cool Way of Preservation

Where Summum's selling point is that the preserved body will serve as a reference point for the soul, "allowing communication of instructions that will help guide you to your new destination," Arizona-based Alcor, the leading name in cryonics, holds out the possibility of here-and-now (well, here-and-later) resurrection.

Cooled by liquid nitrogen to a temperature of -320°F (-196°C), your tissue won't deteriorate, even after centuries. Theoretically it should be possible to reverse your condition and restore good health; human sperm and even embryos are similarly frozen before successful use. The major drawback is that when a body is frozen, ice crystals form in the cells, rupturing the walls. Glycerol is employed as a cryoprotectant—as it is in sperm banks—to minimize the damage, and, it's thought, remedial action will be possible . . . someday. The hope is that during this century the emerging science of nanotechnology will build microminiaturized "robots" small enough to be injected into the bloodstream, which will copy themselves and follow a preset program of repair—whether caused by ice crystals, age, or illness. Nanotechnology, some think, will become more important than the microchip is today. There's another drawback to cryonics: cost—upward of $150,000. But if that's out of your league, Alcor offers

 A JAPANESE man who couldn't afford to arrange cryogenic preservation for his dead father put him in a large refrigerator in Yokohama. City officials became aware of the situation and tried to persuade him to have his dad cremated, but he refused, convinced that one day he could come back to life. Everything was fine for 13 years until the man went traveling and failed to pay his electricity bill. At the time the power was cut off, Yokohama was suffering a heat wave. . . .

A Frenchman had his late father injected with antifreeze and placed in a specially constructed freezer in the basement of his family château in western France. In February 2002 he was ordered by a court to defrost his parents—his mother had gone into the freezer 18 years before—and give them a conventional burial. Remi Martinot, who like his doctor dad is fascinated by cryogenics, vowed to appeal.

URBAN MYTH: Walt Disney, who died in 1966, is rumored to be cryogenically preserved. Not so. Walt was cremated, and his ashes were deposited at Forest Lawn in Glendale, California.

"neuro-suspension" for $50,000—head only. Even then there's the problem of the open-ended bill. What happens when the money runs out? It did for the first cryogenically preserved human, Dr. James H. Bedford, a seventy-three-year-old California psychologist frozen in 1967. As the pioneering spirit, however, Alcor has continued to keep him. Others haven't been so lucky— they've been evicted from their tanks.

Cryonics raises other questions. Practically: Are yet-to-be-invented life-restoring procedures wishful thinking? It takes a great leap of faith to believe that a replacement body could be grown from your DNA for your thawed-out head. And why should a future generation bother to bring you back to life? Ethically: Are frozen people dead, which is to say, have they gone into the life-death cycle? If so and they're resurrected, have they got a soul? Or is cryostasis suicide?

In more than three decades only about a hundred people have ended their "first life cycle" in suspension;

IN 1996 British researchers announced work on a "soul catcher" memory chip that, within thirty years, will be able to capture our feelings and thoughts. "By combining this information with a record of a person's genes, we could recreate a person physically, emotionally and spiritually," said Chris Winter, head of the Telecom artificial life team. "This is the end of death—immortality in the truest sense."

a few more have had their tissue samples stored for hoped-for cloning purposes. And about a thousand Americans have agreed to be frozen, which isn't many in a population of 260 million. In the public mind what cryonics is trying to achieve, as someone quotably said, is "like trying to make a cow out of a hamburger." The life-after-death industry isn't what it was. In recent years several cryonics companies have died, and others may not be long for this world.

 ## Day-to-Day Embalming

Pre–twentieth-century embalmers embalmed to last and last. Modern embalmers—except a handful of celebrity undertakings—try to do just enough to keep the client looking natural and get them through the funeral. The majority of Americans and a percentage of Europeans are embalmed, but most people are vague about the details, and some don't know that it happens. Those who'd prefer to leave it that way and remain blissfully unaware of what Jessica Mitford called "slicing, piercing and pickling" should move on at this point.

Don't know what happens, and in buttock-clenching anticipation of reading that removal of the viscera is involved? Unclench—it isn't. What is, however (reclench), is the replacement of the blood with a solution of disinfectant and preservatives.

The modern embalming machine consists of an electric pump with a three-gallon reservoir, which is filled with about eight ounces of a dyed and perfumed solution (mainly formaldehyde but with other ingredients such as glycerine, borax, phenol, and alcohol) diluted with water. This is hooked up to the body through an incision over either the carotid artery (where the neck meets the shoulder) or the femoral artery (where the thigh meets the groin). A second tube is attached

THE funeral trade reports that bodies in the ground are taking longer to decompose. This isn't entirely due to embalming fluid. Our food now contains so many preservatives, we're being, well, preserved.

through another incision over the jugular or subclavian vein, running out into what is termed the "sewer system." The fluid is pumped under low pressure into the artery, forcing the blood out through the vein. Once the vein tube runs clear, the incisions are sutured.

Next, a trocar, a long hollow needle attached to another tube, is inserted into the abdomen to aspirate gases and remove the contents of the entrails under suction, before a preservative chemical is introduced. The entire procedure must be carried out steadily, with frequent drainage, otherwise irreparable swelling to the face can be caused. Postmortem clots throughout the body may lead to uneven distribution of the embalming fluid under the skin surfaces, which can be remedied by hypodermic injection; if the chest cavity has become sunken, it's packed with proprietary cavity filler. Lungs are now aspirated, the windpipe corked, and the nose deep-packed with cotton wool saturated with liquid insecticide. And now—those open casket viewings—the

FUNERAL homes in Louisiana and New York have reported thefts of embalming fluid to make cigarettes that give a high. Soaked in the fluid and then dried, "wets" or "fries," as such cigarettes are called, are showing up in inner cities, upscale neighborhoods, and college campuses.

"A FUNERAL service is a social function at which the deceased is the guest of honor and the center of attraction. . . . A poorly prepared body in a beautiful casket is just as incongruous as a young lady appearing at a party in a costly gown and with her hair in curlers."

—Frederick and Strub, *Principles and Practices of Embalming*

cosmetics are applied: often helpful in disguising leakage of chemicals.

Embalming does leave relatives thinking the deceased looks in the pink, which, incidentally, is the color caused by carbon monoxide poisoning. Embalming isn't a good idea if the deceased died of jaundice: they turn

WAS Princess Diana pregnant when she died in a Paris car crash in 1997? A report commissioned by Harrods boss Mohamed Fayed, the father of Dodi Fayed, who also died, indicates that Princess Diana was "partially embalmed" at 5 A.M. on the morning of her death—a contravention of the normal practice of not carrying out the procedure until after an autopsy. The presence of embalming fluid in a urine sample, tested to show pregnancy, would probably give a "false" positive result. Princess Diana had denied she was carrying Dodi's child.

green, although this can be masked with pastes and heavy cosmetics.

Yet it may not save social embarrassment. At open casket viewings a funeral director may be seen to hover. Should a buildup of gases distend the abdomen or thorax, he can relieve the pressure by opening an anal vent. At a moment of discretion, of course.

 ## Funky Exits

Buried or cremated, the majority of us take our final bow according to the prevailing customs of our culture, our social class, and our religious conviction, or lack of it. But in the West we live (and die) in an age less trammeled by convention than any in immediate history, and we prefer to celebrate a life rather than mourn it—and what the neighbors think isn't a concern. We can choose a coffin of startling garishness or one of eco-friendliness (see Chapter 4)—and go into it wearing fancy dress if we have a fancy (well, Bela Lugosi wore his Dracula cloak), accompanied, even, by a "biographical" computer installed with a chronicle of our life. We can hold a funeral service without benefit of clergy, and growing numbers do, or go the whole hog and organize a DIY funeral—and that can mean everything from constructing the coffin to helping backfill the grave. We can select wildly inappropriate music for the service, say "Wish Me Luck As You Wave Me Goodbye" instead of "Abide with Me." (Actually, in 1999 "Every Breath You Take" by the Police and "My Heart Will Go On" by Céline Dion were the most requested tunes at American funerals, while in Britain, Whitney Houston's "I Will Always Love You" was the rage.) The eulogy can be played strictly for the laughs. Doves or balloons can be released at the graveside, which needn't be in a bland cemetery but in a woodland site. In 1993 there was no such thing in Britain; in January 1996 there were seventeen; now there are 120 and more on the way. Ten percent of all funerals are forecast to be in woodland burial grounds by 2010. It now appeals to many people not to have their final location identified, and many sites simply mark each plot by planting a tree on it. Some sites cater specifically to pagans and New Age followers.

Even a generation or two ago all of this would have been unimaginable.

We can't by law have a DIY cremation, but not escaping the commercial incinerator doesn't mean we have to come away in a tasteful urn, take up a niche in a columbarium, or be "strewed," as the clergy until recently called it, in a garden of remembrance, which is what traditionally happened. Increasingly the ashes go home to pot the roses, grow bonsai, or get scattered somewhere that has memories or meaning. One man in England stipulated that his ashes be scattered on the spot in the park where he first had sex with his wife. Soccer fields and golf courses are big favorites (some sporting venues with their eye on the ball advertise their availability not only for this but also for funeral services). So are the sea and the mountains—enough people want this kind of oneness with nature that numerous specialist companies have sprung up; there's even aloha scattering from a canoe off Hawaii. In 2001 eighty-two-year-old actress Shelley Winters scattered elder sister Blanche on the grave of Marilyn Monroe in Westwood Park Cemetery, Los Angeles. "I wanted my two best friends to be together," she said.

If something more permanent is wanted, we can be integrated into an artificial reef at various locations around the world, turned into customized slabs or

DO you fancy being buried at sea? The option is available to all active, retired, and honorable veterans of the U.S. military and their families, following strict EPA and U.S. Navy or Coast Guard guidelines. As burials at sea services are performed during official maneuvers, family members are not eligible to attend; however, the commanding officer of the ship will send next of kin a personal letter and include photographs or video of the ceremony.

IN 1989 a California professional ash-scatterer had to pay $27 million to 5,000 families after using the ashes to fertilize his farm. In 1997 a California pilot committed suicide after it was discovered that he hadn't scattered the remains for which he'd been paid—another 5,000. Police had to set up a special warehouse where relatives could search for their loved ones.

Early in 2001 a crematorium owner in the hamlet of Noble, Georgia, was arrested after it was found he'd been pocketing the fees for incinerating corpses but dumping them in the surrounding woods instead. The initial search turned up more than 100 bodies, but police believed there could be hundreds more. "This is the worst horror movie you've ever seen," the local coroner said.

sculptures (in the manner that D. H. Lawrence's wife Frieda had his ashes mixed with concrete for a new mantelpiece), or combined with wood pulp to produce the pages of a bound volume that the firm offering the service calls a "bibliocadaver." More intimate possibilities are suggested by the Frenchman who had his ashes stirred into the paints used in a posthumous portrait for his family; the Florida widower who had his wife's ashes made up into capsules that he consumed, one a day, like multivitamins; or the Australian widow who, when her husband Dustin died in a road accident, had his ashes sewn into her breast implants to keep him close to her heart ("Ashes to ashes, Dustin to dust").

We can even go with a dramatic flourish, packed into cartridges or fireworks—though perhaps, in the latter case, not as dazzlingly as the fireworks showman Vic Vickers ("The Wizard of Aaahs"), who in 1997 became part of the Fourth of July display over Orlando's Lake Eola. If our ambition goes further and we can afford it, we could contact Celestic, Inc., the first company to send cremated remains into orbit. By spring 2001 four missions had been launched. Among those taking the *Earthview Service* were the former Harvard psychologist and LSD guru Timothy Leary, dropping out just as far as he could, and *Star Trek* creator Gene Roddenberry. Dr. Eugene Shoemaker of comet fame was a passenger on the first *Lunar Service.* Yet to come is the *Voyage Service,* which will send ashes into deep space. It's a shame Roddenberry couldn't wait to boldly go on that one.

BURIAL GROUNDS, COFFINS, AND MONUMENTS

 The One-Upmanship of Death

Death is the great equalizer, but in death some are more equal than others. Where you were buried, in what container, and under what marker were once, perhaps, a signal to those accepting delivery in the afterlife that here was someone deserving of preferential treatment. There was also the subtext: the signal to the living of the social worth not only of the departed but of the bereaved.

Rulers in the ancient world looked at, or heard

about, the tomb of King Mausolus in Asia Minor—
which stood eighteen stories high and was crowned
with a sculpted chariot atop a pyramid—and were filled
with a desire to outdo it. Whether they succeeded is
another matter; this, after all, was one of the seven
wonders, an X-marks-the-spot of such impact that
Mausolus's name has given us the word for the kind of
funerary stonemasonry that hits you in the eye.

Big makes a statement. That was so as long ago as
the Neolithic period, when thousands of burial structures in Britain and along the Atlantic seaboard of western Europe were being constructed of vertical slabs of
between twenty and a hundred tons; scholars estimate
that it took a thousand workers eight years full time to
finish the largest. But nothing comes bigger than the
Egyptian pyramids, in particular the Great Pyramid of
Cheops, which may have taken a hundred thousand
men thirty years. Rising forty-eight stories above the
desert, measuring over 7,500 feet along each side of its
base, made up of 2.3 million blocks, it weighs 5.7 million tons and was designed so that the pharaoh in occupation could ascend to the sky up one of its smooth
sides like a water-ski ramp.

In terms of big, no one has come close. But the
Argentine dictator Juan Perón might have tried. The
mausoleum he planned for his Eva was to have been

WHEN Elizabeth, the wife of poet-painter Dante Gabriel Rossetti, died in 1862, her heartbroken husband wrapped a bundle of his unpublished poems in her long tresses to be buried with her—as big a statement of love as he could make. Seven years later when Rossetti, an alcoholic and morphine addict, found the creative flow faltering, he had Elizabeth dug up and retrieved his work.

bigger than Cheops's and would have cost $75 million (at 1952 prices), with a statue of her twice the height of the Statue of Liberty outside and a life-size one in jade inside. Naturally, it's easier to think this big when you're intending to use other people's money—which Perón's overthrow prevented him from doing.

The after-death statement in stone is one that countries are drawn to making on behalf of their elite dead and the vainglorious on behalf of themselves. It's a weakness seemingly inherent in humankind, often running counter to religious conviction. According to original Islamic thought and scripture, graves were to be level with the ground. That didn't last long: as early as the second century of Islam (roughly the eighth in the Western calendar) Muslims were into mausolea like everyone else. Postrevolutionary France, which rationalized God out of existence and proclaimed all citizens equal in death as in life, quickly returned to erecting chunky memorial piles for the great and the good. You have only to look, for instance, at the huge sarcophagus tombs of the Napoleonic generals clustered together in the Parisian cemetery of Père Lachaise to conclude that man's ego always proves bigger than his principles.

One-upmanship in death takes many forms. Aristocrats bagged the best places in church or churchyard next to saints or their relics, or to the altars. When the Church of Scotland banned intramural burial, the landed gentry stumped up the cash to add bogus "aisles" to their places of worship so that they could continue to remain inside. Very Orthodox Jews pay through the nose to secure a spot in Israel's Mount of Olives cemetery (especially if it is next to an important rabbi) because they believe that's where the resurrection will start on Judgment Day—and the first shall be first. Just as in the nineteenth century the fashionable French tried to wangle a plot next to the famous in the new-style cemeteries, so celebrity-conscious

EVER since the aristocracy were wiped out by the Black Plague in the fourteenth century, Norway has had a law that all tombstones must be of the same height.

Angelenos pay big bucks to get into Westwood Village Memorial Park. As Conrad Hilton said about hotels, only three things matter: location, location, location.

Actually, in the one-upmanship of death other things can matter too, and nothing may be too small. Ordinary Victorians even vied with each other over how many studs a coffin had. One thing that has mattered, often in a magnified way, has been whom to be buried among; the lion may lie down with the lamb, but the dead won't necessarily lie down with others of a different race, ethnicity, or religion. In 1999, just as a fence separating blacks and whites was coming down in Jasper, Texas, another in Tynan in the same state was going up to separate the German-American section from the Hispanic-American section.

At least cemeteries are no longer segregated by professional class . . . probably. That was the nineteenth-century practice in the very best cemeteries such as Père Lachaise, the Zentralfriedhof in Vienna, and Brookwood Necropolis in England. Up to the Second World War, Brookwood had its own private railway from York Street at Waterloo, with hearse vans taking London's deceased down to the Surrey countryside. Coffins were segregated by class and profession and were unloaded at one of the cemetery's two stations:

one for Anglicans, the other for Catholics, Jews, and dissidents.

Most people these days aren't bothered about big burial statements—they prefer to overshoot their credit card limit for a quickly forgotten pleasure today rather than for remembrance tomorrow. Those of another mind might heed the words of Diogenes. One day Alexander the Great saw him staring at a pile of bones and asked him what he was looking for. "That which I cannot find," the philosopher replied, "the difference between your father's bones and those of his slaves."

Rise and Fall of the Churchyard

After cave burials, early humankind moved to burying its dead in chambers cut out of rock—as in the Valley of the Kings near Thebes in Egypt, in Petra (present-day Jordan) and in Etruria (Italy); or in mounds of earth or stone or both—as in the barrows of northern Europe, the beehive tombs of Mycenae, the stupas of India, or the hummocks left by the mound builders of Ohio and Mississippi.

Which came first: the city or the cemetery? Despite the fact that the very first townships in Mesopotamia ten thousand years ago buried their dead in brick-built

IN many cultures a woman who died in childbirth was blamed for their own death and denied a proper burial. Mesopotamian cultures also refused burial to a woman who'd had an abortion. The Nuer of the Sudan, who normally practice burial, leave stillborn twins in the fork of a tree. Traditionally in Christianity, stillborn babies did not get funerals because they weren't baptized, but since Victorian times many clergy have ignored this. Only a mother and child or twin children who die together can be buried or cremated together.

spaces under their houses, it's generally agreed that "cities of the dead" came ahead of cities of the living. Food gathering and hunting don't encourage permanent occupation of a single site; dying does. And to be near its dead, humankind had to put down roots. Most urbanized civilizations have chosen to do so adjacent to, not on top of, their dead.

The Greeks and Romans strung their burial sites along the roads leading to their cities. This was because they recognized the burial ground's potential for spreading disease. Early Christians, grown used to spending their religious lives hiding among the dead in the catacombs, and twitchy after a few centuries of Roman persecution, forgot the importance of hygienic measures.

By the Middle Ages, before the practice of putting up tombstones and the like had developed, the graveyards attached to churches were social centers used for markets and fairs, sporting events, archery practice, and gambling. They were so much a part of daily life that even when the Black Death was laying waste to the population, it didn't occur to anyone that trampling about on the newly dead—shallowly buried, in shrouds—spread contagion.

Before the sixteenth century the bones of the dead were frequently moved out of their graves to ossuaries and charnel houses, making way for more customers. But the concept of permanent grave ownership took hold, the epidemics didn't abate, urbanization continued, and the result was graveyard gridlock. The graveyards of the seventeenth century were littered with bones and bits of charnel, scattered by rats and dogs,

THE catacombs were old quarries from which the Romans had dug soft rock called tufa for mortar. Stretching for 350 miles around Rome, they became the burial place for pagans, Jews, and Christians—eventually more than half a million bodies. Another labyrinth of worked-out quarries became the resting place for the exhumed bones of several million people when the French closed the graveyards of Paris.

and were as crammed as rush-hour trains. Putrefying corpses gave out exhalations and darkened the air with vapors. It was virtually impossible to bury one body without digging up another. After the Great Plague of 1665 the English Parliament finally came to the conclusion that graveyards were a problem, banned their use for other activities, and ordered graves to be no less than six feet deep.

The legislation was impossible to implement—so many bodies were going into so few places that one level of burials had to be covered with soil to take the next lot, and then the next. The diarist John Evelyn described the churchyards of London as being so "filled up with the congestion of dead bodies . . . that the churches seemed to be built in pits." And in these churches, with the soil up to the windows and the walls oozing damp, the congregation worshiped, all but overlooked by the congregation of the dead on the other side of the walls. Conditions drove the middle classes to follow the rich and buy their way into intramural buri-

MUSLIM graves are dug deep enough for the deceased to be able to sit up when questioned by the angels, who will report on the life they've led.

WHEN the Church of St. Augustine-the-Less in Bristol was excavated in the 1980s, 107 private vaults were uncovered.

als in every possible space that the church could stuff them.

The Great Fire of London that destroyed most of the city offered a great opportunity for change. John Evelyn and Christopher Wren, who would design St. Paul's Cathedral, argued for large cemeteries outside the city and drew up magnificent plans. Vested clerical interests ensured nothing happened. Arguments rumbled on into the nineteenth century, and things got worse as people packed into the expanding cities created by the Industrial Revolution. Cesspits overflowed into drinking water, open sewers stank, and typhus, typhoid, dysentery, and diphtheria haunted the tenements of the poor. And in their midst the churchyards were filled with rotting bodies. Some rotting bodies were even more in their midst—in the very rooms lived in by families unable to pay for a funeral or afraid of body snatchers (see Chapter 6) or both. Some families kept their dead for days or even weeks and, ignorant of germs, kissed them repeatedly—the kiss of death, indeed. The smell of graveyards was so terrible, it was said that gravediggers "were almost drunkards by force." Critics talked of the "putrid fever," of the "mephitic gases," of the "livid heaps of quarried flesh." A parliamentary investigating committee reported that London had almost two hundred acres of graveyards and fifty thousand bodies were being shoehorned into them every year. Dickens wrote about the state of things in several novels and published a poem in his *Household Words* magazine:

I saw from out the earth peep forth
The white and glistening bones,
With jagged ends of coffin planks,
That e'en the worm disowns;
And once a smooth round skull rolled on,
Like a football, on the stones.

"Garden Cemeteries" and Beyond

When is a burial ground a cemetery and not a churchyard? When it isn't attached to a church is the obvious answer, although many cemeteries have chapels (when is a chapel not a church?), and when the chapel is large and the cemetery small, the distinction blurs.

The first major cemeteries were established in the

CHURCHYARDS are still in use in alpine and central European regions where the land can't be extended. These are regularly cleared of bones for storage.

eighteenth century by the Danes, Dutch, and English in India, and by the Americans, for the very reason that Europe was choosing to ignore—alarming death rates. In Europe the Swedes were the first to prohibit burials inside churches. When France followed toward the end of the century, it created "garden cemeteries" with plentiful trees and shrubs, returning to what the Greeks and Romans had done two thousand years ago—organize the burial grounds outside city limits.

Elsewhere in Europe, as cemeteries replaced churchyards, they tended to replicate continental living, albeit with classical influences, providing "apartment blocks" of loculi for the dead in galleries and vaults. Walled and cloistered, many cemeteries in southern Europe suggest that the residents are enjoying a genteel exclusivity.

While Scotland and Ulster replaced churchyard with cemetery burial as quickly as the French, the English stubbornly carried on in the old way for another fifty years. To be strictly accurate, a number of small cemeteries were formed during that time by a mixture of dis-

URBAN MYTH: Mozart wasn't buried in a pauper's grave in 1791. He received a "third-class" funeral, which wasn't unusual in Vienna at the time. And he was buried in a coffin, not a shroud. Outrage has been expressed that the great musician had no one at his funeral, but that was common. Continental Europe had established cemeteries, but people still remembered the horrific conditions of the old graveyards, and funerals remained unattended.

senters and nonconformists, whose reasons had more to do with the rejection of the established Church of England than with hygiene.

It took a ferocious series of cholera epidemics in the middle of the nineteenth century for the English to get the message collectively and close the graveyards. This was at the height of Victorian romanticism; thus the new cemeteries were declared to have the high-minded purpose of being not only burial grounds but open-air art galleries and botanical gardens. How this differed from what the French had already done is difficult to see, but the English are always able to take a superior position.

Having experienced the same problems as everyone else with intramural and graveyard burial, the United States developed garden cemeteries at the same time as France (and they're regarded as superior, whatever

IT'S not impossible to get buried in an English church-yard—just nearly impossible. In 2002 the vicar of a church in Scarborough had a few vacancies and asked all parishioners over the age of fifty if they wanted to be considered. In the same year in Romania, where burial plots are scarce, a family denied admittance left the body of an elderly relative on a table outside the church. The priest relented and buried it, but then had to mount a guard for fear competitors for the plot might dig it up.

the French say). But a series of epidemics in the early twentieth century galvanized a further move forward—the memorial park. The concept was that of Dr. Hubert Easton, who envisaged a place "devoid of misshapen monuments and other signs of earthly death, but filled with towering trees, sweeping lawns, splashing fountains, beautiful statuary and memorial architecture."

Not unlike the garden cemetery? Actually, it was nothing like the garden cemetery—if you discount the

IN 1918 the U.S. death toll from the flu epidemic—responsible for a third of the nation's deaths in that year, cutting life expectancy from 50.9 to 39.1—was so great, a coffin shortage occurred.

THE U.S. now has drive-in cemeteries for those seeking to reconcile devotion to the dead with other pressing engagements.

controlled nature—as was seen at Forest Lawn in Glendale, near Los Angeles, which opened in 1928 with wedding chapels, concert halls, a cinema, art galleries (housing copies of famous works of art and exhibiting the world's largest painting of the crucifixion, 197 by 43 feet), and other attractions. Although lampooned by Evelyn Waugh in *The Loved One,* derided by Mitford, and generally sneered at as a Disneyland of the dead, the memorial park continues to oust the traditional cemetery in America, which suggests it touches a fundamental need unrecognized by traditionalists.

The British and continental Europeans may well balk at naming areas of burial ground Whispering Pines, Everlasting Love, Kindly Light, or Babyland. But as to the wedding chapels, theaters and the rest—why not? Why not, as suggests the poet-undertaker Thomas Lynch, who plies his trade in Milford, Michigan, create a "golfatorium," which requires no explanation? The Middle Ages didn't get it entirely wrong. And the Japanese and Mexicans continue to use their cemeteries as festive places on certain occasions connected with honoring the dead. Is the *fun* in *funeral* for nothing?

Modern population growth is putting the pinch on cemeteries and memorial parks. "Necrotecture" seeks to maximize the usage of space—one set of graves

SOME cemeteries are tourist attractions, including Highgate in north London, opened in 1839 as the first modern-style cemetery in Britain, and Brookwood Necropolis, the largest in the country—9,500 acres, a quarter of a million bodies. In Europe, others include Père Lachaise in Paris and the Zentralfriedhof in Vienna. In America tourists visit Mount Auburn near Boston, the first garden cemetery in the U.S., the cemeteries of New Orleans, where, unusually, the graves are above ground (New Orleans is below sea level), and of course Glendale—and the four other Forest Lawns in California. In India, South Park Street, Calcutta, established in 1767 after the "sick season" carried off large numbers of Europeans, pulls in the visitors.

Europe's most populated cemetery is the City of London cemetery at Wanstead in east London, with half a million burials, but the largest in the world is Rookwood in Sydney—700 acres, 600,000 bodies, 2,000 cremated remains.

Several tours in Hollywood will take you to the places where various stars met their sudden end. Interest in such matters has been termed "dark tourism."

THE Franco-Prussian War in the 1870s and the American Civil War in the 1860s led to a new kind of consecrated ground: the military cemetery. The British War Commission, established in 1917 by royal charter, maintains the graves of the members of the Commonwealth forces killed in the two world wars. There are Commonwealth war graves in 12,500 military cemeteries in fifty different countries.

The Arlington National Cemetery in Virginia, across the Potomac River from Washington, D.C., buries those who served in the U.S. armed forces. Although it covers six hundred acres, it has few spaces left. John F. Kennedy and William Howard Taft are the only presidents buried there. The Tomb of the Unknown Soldier contains the unidentified remains of a soldier from each of the two world wars and the Korean War. Since 1948 the tomb has been guarded twenty-four hours a day.

twelve feet under, another on top, six feet under, an expeditious solution employed unhygienically and haphazardly in the seventeenth century. In Britain up to six burials are allowed in one eight-foot-square plot, but it depends on the type of ground—gravel is favored for its drainage but makes deep digging difficult. Usually the first two coffins are placed side by side; later ones go in on top. Plots are usually doubles (husband and wife), but you can buy singles. Anyone unable to afford to pay is buried by the local council in a "common grave"—a stranger may already be in it or join you later. Another move in some places is toward community mausolea, derided by purists as "tenements," which popularly stack burial spaces six or eight high on either side of a visitors' corridor. There's a limit to how deep you can dig to bury the dead, but with upward expansion the sky's the limit.

Buried Under What Marker?

The great cemeteries of the nineteenth century look like a scaled-down combination of Greek, Roman, and Egyptian architecture with, here and there in miniature, structures that Hollywood imagined to dot medieval England—and a few that could have been inspired by the scarier side of *Lord of the Rings.*

From medieval times some free-standing tombs were placed in ecclesiastical buildings, but during the seventeenth and eighteenth centuries, the period that saw the rise of the urban middle class with spending

 WEALTHY Roman families would often sell space in their mausoleum to the middle class who couldn't afford such grand funerary monuments on their own.

power, so many went up that cathedrals, churches, and chapels came to resemble indoor cemeteries. The fashion of erecting tons of stone and marble in memory of those lying beneath the flags started with the Dutch who, like other Europeans, had been astonished by the opulence of tombs in India and went into me-too mode. It spread to England when William of Orange came to rule, and the sweep and spatial design of many places of worship were spoiled by monumental clutter. But there's no standing in the way of fashion.

Carved, embellished, decorated, and inscribed, the monuments of all ages are important pieces of funerary history. They can also be masterpieces when from the hand of the likes of Michelangelo and da Vinci. But all those nooks and crannies are awful dust collectors. That wasn't what ended their era, of course; the end of church and churchyard burial did. Yet there was a final flourish before the wealthy moved off to prime spots in the new cemeteries: English landowners, the nouveau

 ROADSIDE memorials: In the last few years the practice of placing flowers at the sites of fatal accidents has grown. The older custom of donating memorial benches to local parks is so popular that some councils have dozens that they don't know what to do with.

riche among them, took to erecting their mausolea in the parks of their estates. These were the first built outdoors in Britain since Roman times—and the ultimate segregation from the common herd.

The demise of the "statement" burial monument is mourned by antiquarians, who feel that a richness has gone from human experience; that the utilitarian flat metal markers in American memorial parks reduce the dead to a roll call; and that the unmarked graves of many woodland sites are almost as soulless as cremation—which they consider worse, however, because it robs the bereaved of a focus for their grief and consolation. Many traditionalists find contemporary funerary design depressing or in dubious taste; according to one, "the uninspired tombstones or memorials erected today have added new terrors to death." So there.

It's a matter that can be debated; we're all creatures of our time. In northern Europe during the Black Death and later, funerary monuments contrasted earthly splendor and decay with realistic relish, depicting corpses being devoured by rats, worms, and snails, and effigies with the incisions and stitches made by the embalmers. The Victorians painted many monuments garish colors, the cherubs' pink faces being set off by cream stone and red and black lettering.

The declining number of people who still choose

THE first U.S. "cemeteries" in cyberspace, such as www.worldgardens.com and Plan4ever.com's Virtual Gardens give those whose loved ones have been cremated "a place to grieve." Relatives and friends can write an obituary, add a picture, or show video clips. Such sites are also popular in Europe and Japan.

burial are no more or less tasteful, whether they're thin echoes of classicism, rampant with Victorian sentimentality (the Victorians really were obsessed with angels), the kind of rococo confections favored by those of Greek and Russian Orthodox or Latinate Catholic persuasion, or feature household appliances, such as wheelbarrows or baby buggies. And who's to say the green chips and the plastic flowers detract from fond remembrance? A fairly recent trend is toward incorporating photographs into the stonework—though you might draw the line at the fad among Russian mafiosi for life-size ones in color, wearing Hawaiian shirts.

Rest in (Disturbed) Peace

In the U.K. and the U.S. we purchase graves in perpetuity and tend to think of them as places of permanent residence, but history is against us. Even new cemeteries built outside city limits are swallowed by urban expansion and "decommissioned." San Francisco is the prime example. It grew at such a rate in the 1930s and 1940s that its cemeteries were closed and their occupants moved on—as had already happened after the 1849 Gold Rush. In all, ninety thousand departed San Franciscans departed again for Colma, five miles to the south. It's now illegal to operate a cemetery or crematorium in Frisco; and Colma has the distinction of having more dead residents (about a million) than live (fifteen hundred). The possibility that cemetery residents will lose their lease becomes greater when a cemetery is full; once new arrivals stop, a new road scheme or housing development can seem a more pressing need to the living.

In Britain the purchase of a certificate of grant entitles the holder to a grave plot for a maximum of fifty years. On expiration it may be renewed for a further term, subject to prevailing circumstances. Some continental cemeteries operate a similar system—Père Lachaise has announced it won't kick out rock star Jim Morrison, whose thirty-year tenure was up in 2002—but on the whole being more practical about such matters, they lease grave plots for shorter periods and spaces in loculi and columbaria for shorter times still. Across the continent leases are realistically set to cover upkeep; once expired, the bones are stored.

TOMBSTONE, Cochise County, southeastern Arizona, U.S.: The site was ironically named by Ed Schieffelin, who discovered silver there in 1877 after being told that all he would find would be his tombstone. By 1881 a silver rush had set in, bringing an estimated seven thousand people to the area. Along with the prospectors came adventurers and outlaws, among whom were Doc Holliday and Johnny Ringo, whereupon Tombstone gained a reputation for lawlessness. Feuds were common, the most notable being the gun battle at the OK Corral in 1881 between the Earp and Clanton families. The boom days quickly ended with floodwaters in the mines, labor strikes, and low silver prices. Tombstone is now a tourist center and health resort and retains a pioneer atmosphere. It was declared a National Historic Landmark in 1962. Restored sites include Boot Hill Cemetery, Bird Cage Theater, the OK Corral, and the *Tombstone Epitaph* Office.

—*Encyclopaedia Britannica*

The remains of the famous are even more likely to be disturbed than others'. Dante's, for instance, went back and forth between Florence and Ravenna according to shifting political fortunes. Rousseau, Napoleon, and British-American political activist Thomas Paine are among the countless figures who have been reburied to mark political change. Entirely for reasons of prestige the bodies of many celebrated people, including

Beethoven and Schubert, were transferred to the Viennese Zentralfriedhof when it opened, as happened at Père Lachaise. If Jim Morrison is in a position to be interested, reburials nearby include the twelfth-century lovers Abelard and Héloïse, La Fontaine and Molière, and Oscar Wilde, rescued from obscurity in Bagneaux, which he must have hated.

There was something of a shuttle service of reburials during the 1980s and 1990s. The composer Béla Bartók left New York for Budapest, and pianist and politician Jan Paderewski left Arlington for Warsaw. The Hungarians brought home József Cardinal Mindszenty, who'd spent twenty-five years either in jail or in political asylum before his death in exile in Austria. The Sioux chief Long Wolf returned home from London to South Dakota.

Wanting to inhume the famous dead, even belatedly, among "their own" is an atavistic human need, but there can be kudos in laying claim, for other reasons, to some remains. When Che Guevara's grave was found

GRAVES and their contents tell us much of what we know about the past. For instance, an examination of the bones of eighty-seven women buried in an English crypt between 1729 and 1852 indicates that modern women's bones are thinner.

in South America, three different countries demanded his body. His daughter gave him to Cuba.

 ## Where Are the Famous Buried?

There are tens of thousands of cemeteries around the world, and any one worth its reputation has someone famous in it. The greatest concentration of those made famous by the twentieth century is in the cemeteries of southern California. But the major cathedrals of the world are the great repositories of the dead, not just across time but in the diversity of those taken to their bosom.

More than three thousand celebrated men and women are interred, for instance, in Westminster Abbey, including many English kings and queens, from Edward the Confessor nearly a thousand years ago to George II in 1760. Since then deceased royals have taken up residence in Windsor Castle (where Henry VIII is, with Jane Seymour, whom he didn't behead).

The abbey is crowded with names: musicians, actors, scientists, politicians, explorers—Handel, Purcell, Garrick, Irving, Olivier, Newton, Darwin, both Pitts, Gladstone, Livingstone—as well as engineers, architects, military men, and many more. Poets' Corner in the abbey reads like a roll call of English literature: Chaucer, Spenser,

Dryden, Johnson, Dickens, Browning, Tennyson, Kipling, Masefield—the last man of letters, who died in 1967.

In one respect the Elizabethan poet Ben Jonson is the most fascinating internee. One story has it that, dying in poverty, he begged eighteen inches of ground in the abbey from Charles I; another that he begged two feet from the dean (perhaps he'd grown stouter). Whichever, if either, is true, Jonson is the only person in Westminster Abbey to be buried standing upright, beneath the nave.

Whose are the most visited graves in the world is fiercely debated. As far as Americans are concerned, John F. Kennedy's in Arlington, with wife Jackie and brother Robert nearby, is the favorite: nearly five million tourists are drawn there every year. Elsewhere, Jim Morrison and Oscar Wilde draw the crowds at Père Lachaise in Paris, Karl Marx in Highgate, London, Bruce Lee (and son Brandon) in Lake View, Seattle, and Bob Marley in Rhoden Hall, Nine Mile, fifty miles north of Kingston, Jamaica. Morrison's grave has a life-size bust; Marx's is so massive that it dominates his corner of Highgate. The Lees' grave is simple, even stark; Marley's, only feet from the small stone house where he was born, has a sizable mausoleum—and even more sizable stage behind it. Wilde's memorial was commissioned from the sculptor Jacob Epstein, took three

ONCE you'd have had to search biographies to find where the famous are buried; now on the Net you can find almost all of them at the move of a mouse. Famous Graves at www.findagrave.com has a searchable database of 3.1 million. Other similar sites include www.geocities.com, which covers the 1980s to the present; www.seeing-stars.com and www.genealogyspot.com are both devoted to Hollywood. The Net is an Aladdin's cave of other people's obsessions. Where gravesites are concerned, there are websites devoted to famous Germans, famous economists(!), famous politicians (graves, cremations, and burials at sea)—and many more.

years to complete, and featured an anatomically complete Egyptian male figure, which when it was unveiled in 1912 the cemetery conservator deemed indecent. A fig-leaf plaque was fashioned, but ten years later it was removed by person or persons unknown acting so hastily that more than was intended went with it.

 Buried in What Container?

Across time, when bodies weren't being laid directly in the earth, they were buried in "chests" of wood, baked clay, or stone. In the Middle Ages such chests were of lead. By Elizabethan times the rich were being buried in wooden coffins, and often the poor made their last jour-

IN 1580 the port of Rye in Sussex, England, passed a law that required the purchase of a license if a body was to be buried in a coffin.

ney in a reusable "parish coffin," which came back to the church when its shrouded occupant went into the grave. The widespread use of wooden coffins dates back only two hundred years, when they came within reach of ordinary people.

The development of industrial technology in the nineteenth century saw the introduction of other materials, including glass, cement, celluloid, india rubber, and metal. The last did not go unchallenged: the right to bury a corpse in a coffin of iron came before Lord Stowell in London, who ruled in favor of the protesting churchwardens on the grounds that in conventional wood "the dissolution of bodies is accelerated and the dangerous virulence of the fermentation disarmed by a speedy absorption of the noxious particles into the surrounding soil."

Enthusiasts of metal were not dissuaded, particularly in the United States. In the 1920s the catalog of a funeral merchandiser in Chicago read:

When Robert Fulton said he could propel a boat by steam his friends were sure he was mentally deranged—that it could not be done. When Benjamin Franklin said he could draw electricity from the clouds his acquaintances thought he was crazy—that it could not be done. When our designing and manufacturing department said they could and would produce a cast bronze casket . . . their friends and associates shook their heads sympathetically, feeling that it would be a hopeless task. All three visions have come to be realities—the steamboat, electricity, and the Hilco Peerless Cast Bronze Receptacle.

By the 1960s metal was de rigueur in the United States, outselling wood. So popular was it that even crematoria accepted lightweight ones, which buckled and partially melted—and sometimes caused the deceased to be baked rather than combusted. Environmental concerns have meant a return to wood as the material of choice, though metal and fiberglass are still favored precisely because they don't biodegrade, "thereby protecting the body from the environment, and the environment from the body, for countless tomorrows."

There has been a big change in the United States (and to a lesser extent in some other places) in attitudes as to what a burial box should look like. Forget polished wood if you wish: blue, crimson, emerald green, and pewter tones are available; as are leopard-print coffins, custom-made coffins shaped like Cadillacs or surf-boards, chrome-edged coffins for Harley-Davidson buffs, human-shaped coffins like ancient Egyptian *suhets*. (Don't forget the Summum Mummiform for the permanently embalmed, which can come in gold rather than bronze or steel, with inlaid jewels and a "life mask" of the occupant's face.) An Australian company on its website says, "We offer people the chance to be as imaginative in death as they are in life, by choosing a coffin or casket that makes a statement about who and what they are." While not serving the international market, the Ga of Ghana, especially in the village of Teshi, have gained a reputation for making wooden coffins in fanciful shapes—fish, birds, and mammals to Bibles and bicycles—and in bright colors, to suit the person-ality of the deceased.

For the conservative who nonetheless finds the tradi-tional container a bit humdrum, the market offers models

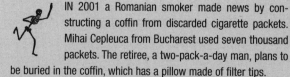

IN 2001 a Romanian smoker made news by con-structing a coffin from discarded cigarette packets. Mihai Cepleuca from Bucharest used seven thousand packets. The retiree, a two-pack-a-day man, plans to be buried in the coffin, which has a pillow made of filter tips.

with more oomph—carved or painted, not just outside but inside too. The Last Supper is the United States' best seller, but nature scenes, sunbursts, and school and other crests are very popular. The best-selling model put out by a company in Slovenia—a major supplier to Croatia, Germany, Austria, and Hungary—offers a carved Christ. Scene-carving in modern times is an innovation, but what goes around comes around: the Romans moved from cremation to burial in the second century largely because the sarcophagus reemerged with elaborate carvings that showed your life accomplishments.

While modern influences have begun to appear in European coffin design, the coffin retains its discreet shape: narrow at the head, wider at the shoulder, and tapering toward the feet, fitting the form within it. The American coffin, on the other hand—usually referred to as a casket, though the terms are frequently interchangeable—is rectangular and approximately the size of a refrigerator.

But, if anything, Chinese coffins, traditionally made of four half-logs and weighing up to three hundred pounds, are bigger. The Chinese often buy their coffins decades in advance and have them ready, a fact that stimulated contributors to the *Times* of London a few years ago: one deemed it an excellent idea but wondered, considering that so many people live in apartments and storage is a problem, whether the coffin had to be propped up in the hall; another suggested that the item could be a convertible cocktail cabinet, coat closet, or grandfather clock, which might "prove to be the most popular and appropriate retirement present of all."

The Eco Argument

Most nineteenth-century reformers advocated cremation but as an alternative recommended coffins of paper or wicker or ones with sides that could be removed once lowered into the grave. By and large they met with indifference if not hostility from those who wanted to preserve the body from decay.

A hundred or more years later the Western world had come around to such thinking. In Britain now more than a dozen companies sell inexpensive biodegradable enclosures ranging from cloth bags to wicker burial stretchers and coffins of woven willow, bamboo, papier mâché, and cardboard (flat-pack option available). Biodegradable urns can be purchased if cremated remains are to be buried. When the British National Death Centre was launched in 1991 and called for cardboard coffins, only a handful of cemeteries and crematoria was prepared to accept them. That changed within three years. For health and safety reasons some undertakers don't permit staff to carry a cardboard coffin, but will provide a trolley, if you haven't got your own pallbearers.

The United States is a long way behind the UK on the issue of environmentally friendly burial, but at least the sale of metal coffins—200 million pound' weight per year—is in decline.

For a decade Americans have been able to rent a top-of-the-line "show" or chapel coffin but have the burial conducted in something cheaper. (Some undertakers have introduced the facility in Britain, but the demand is slight.) Such coffins are made with an inner container that can go into another coffin if desired—but which is suitable for "eco" burial or cremation as it is.

There are no laws about coffins, even homemade ones.

Cremation is less damaging to the environment than coffin burial, but it does emit dioxins, hydrochloric and hydrofluoric acids, sulfur dioxide, and carbon dioxide. Pine is recommended for cremation (with combustible brass-colored plastic fittings) rather than hardwood, which requires more energy to burn, but cardboard and

"WITH our chapel casket we have chosen to use traditional solid oak caskets which sell for a much higher price. If you are comparing rental fees elsewhere, be sure to ascertain what quality of casket the other firm is using, and what the difference is between their rental cost and purchase price. You'll find that ours gives much more value for the dollars spent."—U.S. brochure

other delicate materials require the least energy and produce the fewest pollutants.

Coffin burial pollutes the soil through the breakdown of solvents, glue, and finishes—and the leakage of embalming fluid. It's also responsible for the destruction of rain forests. According to the Rainforest Action Group, loggers waste twenty-eight hardwood trees for every one they harvest for coffin making, which in the United States takes between 150 and 225 board-feet of wood per coffin—between 41 and 68 million board-feet a year.

If you're environmentally conscious, then not being embalmed and going into the earth in a degradable container is the least harmful option. It means you'll contribute to the surroundings more quickly as nature recycles you into trees, plants, or grass.

GERMAN Karl-Friedrich Lentze has won the right to be buried with his blow-up sex doll. "I would like to ask, with all due respect, whether it would be possible to have an inflated sex doll laid to rest with me in the coffin," he wrote to the Bonn council. In March 2002 the council said yes—on condition that the doll is biodegradable.

Rise of the Undertaker—
The "Dismal Trader"

If you DIY the funeral, you can take the undertaker out of the loop, but few people, in fact, do—undertaking undertaking would unnerve most of us.

Up until the eighteenth century, burial needed the input of several different workers: the local carpenter (or sometimes cabinetmaker), who made the coffin; the livery stable keeper, who provided the hearse and funeral carriage; and the sexton, who looked after gravedigging and bell-tolling. The first undertakers rolled these services into one—they "undertook" them, supplying the coffin from their own workplace or from a catalog, bringing the folding chairs (the service was frequently held at home), taking charge of the pallbearers, and seeing to it that the body reached the grave. It was a step toward respectability, but a small one; undertaking was a trade and a downmarket one at that. (In some countries it's still assigned to those considered of lower caste, such as the Untouchables in India and the *Eta* in Japan.) By the start of the nineteenth century, "dismal traders" were held in contempt in Britain, as were others connected with the burial business. The chaos and the horrifying conditions that existed had given rise to wholesale corruption, fake clergymen offering to officiate at funeral services, exorbitant fees, fraudulent burial clubs, and the disposal of the freshly dead (with axes, saws, and furnaces) to free up scarce spots. Many coffins went back to the undertaker for resale, as did handles—even coffin nails.

In the United States, a bigger, younger country, the undertaker was free of this unsavoriness. And shortly before the end of the nineteenth century, he conferred upon himself the title of "funeral director" and thereby joined the professional classes. He no longer undertook funerals. He directed—lights, camera, action.

Upwardly mobile, American funeral directors dispensed with their simple local stores. In their place came establishments inspired by English country homes, French châteaux, and Spanish missions. Bodies were inspected in slumber rooms ranging in style from the gothic baroque to the Victorian drawing room, and

IF Nat Fisher, patriarch of the dysfunctional Fisher family in TV's award-winning *Six Feet Under,* had directed the hearse while he was reaching for a crafty cigarette, he would have continued to run his funeral parlor business and not become a client of it.

In the U.K., where audiences also dig the show, the first series' trailers were shown during episodes of *E.R.*—highly appropriate, as tales from the mortuary are evidently post-hospital drama.

There's an actors' joke about hospital drama offering wheel-on parts. The same joke holds good, with the operating table replaced by the slab or casket—and the extras on them know there'll never be any dialogue in a recovery scene. Unlike Nat—but one ghost is enough even for *Six Feet Under.*

chapels of rest were provided, cutting out the clergy as God's middlemen. As Evelyn Waugh put it, the American funeral director became the first to offer eternal salvation at an inclusive charge as part of the service.

 R.I.P.-off?

The burial business has always been open to corruption and malpractice. In the sixteenth and seventeenth centuries, when only royalty, nobility, and the sincerely rich were buried within church precincts, those already in residence were often evicted—for a suitable fee. For three hundred years the clergy resisted changes in burial practices because they provided a nice little livelihood, legal as well as illegal, as they were. Legislation in England to shut the churchyards overcame clerical opposition only by paying compensation to the incumbents of parishes from which corpses were sent off to the new cemeteries.

The American way of death post–Second World War was already under fire before British investigative journalist Jessica Mitford got her aristocratic teeth into it: its "synthetic chapels," where a funeral director instead of a priest "administered empathy and semi-classical music"; its almost universal embalming, which made corpses "look more and more like window-display mannequins"; and its prices, which were "steadily moving the whole industry beyond the reach of satire."

Mitford was abrasive about these aspects but more so about some of the tactics employed, in particular what has since been called the bait-and-switch: the prospective casket buyer first shown the cheaper lines, "so hideous that only customers who can afford the barest minimum will buy them," before being moved on to something more pleasing—and expensive—and shamed into purchase. Another development that raised Mitford's ire was the protective—as opposed to

TWENTY years ago a cremation cost 20% of the price of burial. Nowadays, cremation is still cheaper than burial, but not by that much.

the nonprotective—casket, designed, as one website today typically reads, "to prevent the entrance of grave site elements, like water, soil and air." Caskets range from about $1,000 to $15,000, four to twenty times wholesale, with the steepest markups at the lower end.

The burial vault is a related but separate, uniquely American introduction into the burial business and one of sheer financial genius. An outer receptacle to further protect the protective casket or to give protection to the nonprotective casket, the vault may be of concrete (but pre-asphalt-lined), fiberglass, aluminum, steel, copper, or a composite of concrete, plastic, and copper; they come plain, striped, or otherwise decorated. Vaults weigh up to two thousand pounds, some are designed to resist five thousand pounds of pressure per square inch, and they "get more beautiful every year." And of course, pricier. In 1915 the vault was used in only 5 percent of U.S. burials; by the 1960s it was 60 percent; nowadays most places of burial insist on them to prevent the ground from collapsing—even though an average course of cheap concrete or metal stays, as are used under monuments elsewhere in the West, would do the job.

And all to what purpose? In the fortified dugouts of their tombs, inside their airtight and watertight defenses, generations of Americans lie in a state of unprogressive decay—"repugnant, mouldy, foul-looking objects," a pathologist told Mitford. Gone, but not forgotten . . . but surely better not remembered like that. If permanent preservation is the object of the exercise, why not encase the body in plastic and be done with it?

Funeral directors have been accused, and at times found guilty, of pressuring and bilking the bereaved at a time of intense vulnerability. There have been cases where the bereaved have been fraudulently told that embalming is required by law—though no state re-

IN Taiwan the funeral industry has been infiltrated by criminals who have been taking over private funeral businesses, discouraging free-market competition by threats or outright destruction of competitors' premises, and charging for unneeded services, while failing to do what they've been paid to do. The Taipei city government has taken steps to reduce the influence of organized crime and corruption.

quires it up to seventy-two hours after death, and even after that every state except Minnesota allows the alternative of refrigeration. American burial grounds have

 THE £1 billion British burial business has had its share of accusations of high-pressure salesmanship and overcharging. In 2001 the Office of Fair Trading (OFT) ordered it to make its costs clearer. To help people decide whether undertakers are charging fairly, the OFT has stated that the wholesale price of a veneer oak coffin "is in the region of £35" ($55).

About 70% of funerals in Britain take place under the Funeral Ombudsman Scheme, an independent consumer protection agency.

Some British funeral establishments have led the way toward total transparency by putting their prices online—everything from the cost of an ambulance service per hour to mortuary refrigeration.

Typical prices: biodegradable bodybags, £21 ($33); cardboard coffins direct from the wholesaler, £57 ($89), including overnight delivery; chipboard coffins, £55 ($86). A company in southwest London offers chipboard veneer "without fancy handles or fancy lining . . . using wood from managed sustained-yield forests" for £45 ($70)—free delivery within five miles.

The world's largest producer of eco-friendly coffins is at www.greenundertakings.co.uk.

had their leash pulled, too. In 1935 three-quarters were publicly owned. By the 1960s that was a quarter—and the expensive-to-get-into social-cachet cemeteries and memorial parks with high ongoing-upkeep charges continue to drive out the low-priced municipal and church sites. And as Mitford pointed out forty years ago, homes on reasonable plots come six to the acre, while cemeteries house "1,500 or better."

In 1960 America spent $1.6 billion on its funerals and attendant costs. Now it's $23 billion.

In the wake of Mitford, countless media exposés and stings have brought about changes in U.S. law and new trade practice rules, but while America is said to be trying to bring down its funeral costs and there's been a big rise in memorial societies (cheap coffins, no embalming, no viewing), there's been no seismic shift. Perhaps in a nation of excess, demand drives supply—even when supply manipulates demand. As has been

IN March 2001 seventeen young British artists and fashion designers mounted an exhibition at the Roundhouse in London as a criticism of the funeral industry. They showed coffins that glow in the dark, coffins made from fruit boxes, tiny girl and boy jewel-box fetal coffins, and balloons to catch the dying breath.

pointed out, if the United States were weaned off open casket viewing—the very cornerstone of the American way of death—embalming and the vulgarly exorbitant casket might become redundant.

The biggest force for change in the United States as elsewhere is the Internet. Until a few years ago it would have been impossible to buy a coffin direct; now they're widely available in many countries. Funeral directors still don't like the idea (and charge a "handling fee" for coffins purchased from someone else), but they're finding they don't really have a choice. If they won't meet the demand, someone else with a website will.

The funeral industry may not be as powerful as the gun lobby, but so far it has managed to block attempts to open eco-friendly burial grounds, which could seriously damage its bottom line. How long the situation lasts remains to be seen. In the meantime Americans who own land can legally treat themselves to an environmentally

THE average cost of an American funeral is around $7,800, and the average cost of a British one is just over £2,000—approximately two and a half times less. In Britain the most basic funeral can be held for £318.50 (a government figure). A woodland burial averages £900 and usually includes the tree.

friendly resting place there; and those who don't can be shipped to England (though that necessitates embalming). Again, details can be found on the Internet. Who said the Web was only good for pornography?

 ## The Funeral Service

On his deathbed Voltaire was urged by a priest to renounce the devil. Voltaire replied: "Now is not the time to make new enemies." Most people probably feel like that about undertakers/funeral directors.

In general, anxieties about the funeral industry have arisen where big business has moved in, taken over family firms, and concentrated on increasing margins. You can only hope that the afterlife takes their accounts into account and that the funeral fat cats go into everlasting liquidation. But in the last few years a number of funeral directors in the United States have turned their face against corporate greed and set up in a simple way, offering, if required, to lay out the dead in the family living room or in the church, as was once traditional.

People would prefer to think that so-called "bier barons" aren't angling for their wallets, whatever the later bill; most are grateful for the courteous and unobtrusive service that's usually provided during a period when they feel almost as numb as the deceased. None are more grateful than those who've lost someone in an accident: a skilled mortician can make the disfigured dead presentable, so that loved ones can say good-bye. A missing hand can be replaced with one cast in colored plaster; a missing nose or ear modeled in wax; even decapitation can be addressed. As long ago as 1912 American mortician Joel Crandall performed "demi-surgery" on a young man whose head had been crushed between the buffers of two trains. He made a skull to replace the original, which was in eighty pieces, and restored the features. The contemporary undertaker-poet Thomas Lynch tells of a colleague who labored for a day and a night to piece together the parts of the cranium of a girl who'd been murdered with a baseball bat, so that her mother could see her face again, "not the madman's version."

The undertaker/funeral director isn't someone you think about until you need him (yes, like a plumber). When you do, he's there. In one of his poems Lynch says plainly that in his hometown he has

> *certain duties here. Notably,*
> *when folks get horizontal, breathless, still:*
> *life in Milford ends. They call. I send a car.*

WHEN YOU'VE GOT TO GO . . .

When Will It Happen?

According to an old fable, a man made an agreement with Death: when it came time to die, he would willingly accompany the Grim Reaper, on condition he was sent a messenger well in advance to warn him. One winter evening, Death came. Startled, the man cried out, "You're here so soon and without warning! I thought we had an agreement." Death replied, "Look in the mirror. Once your hair was full and black, now it's thin and white. Look how you cock your head to listen to me because you can't hear very well. Observe how close to the mirror you must stand to see yourself clearly. Yes,

I've sent many messengers through the years. I'm sorry you're not ready, but the time has come to leave."

In mythology, heroes and heroines court death and go to it "as to a bridal bed, and sacrificed themselves to others without remorse at the shrines of love, of honour, or religion, or any other prevailing feeling," as the eighteenth-century essayist William Hazlitt wrote. It may well be true, as Shakespeare said, that cowards die many times before their death and that the "valiant never taste of death but once"; it's certainly true that circumstances can make the most unlikely people self-sacrificially heroic. But most of us are too attached to life to contemplate heroics. Whatever vicissitudes life throws at us, we prefer life to the alternative.

Since the beginning of time seventy billion people

IN 1902 the average age of death in Britain was 43. Today men are nudging 75 and women 80. Worldwide, people over 80 are the fastest-growing segment of the population. They represent only 1.1% but their number has risen by 60% between 1970 and 1998—from 26.7 million to 66 million. The three countries with the highest proportion of over-eighties are Sweden (4.8%), Norway (4.2%), and Britain (4.1%). By 2050 a third of all people in the West will be over 65—and those reaching that age can expect another 17.5 years.

have come and gone. Today, around the world, death—the most terrifying of ills, as Epicurus called it more than two thousand years ago—carries off nearly six thousand people an hour.

When will it happen to you? Who knows? There may be a No. 7 bus coming down the road this minute with your name on it. That aside, antibiotics, vaccinations, life-saving drugs, and medical interventions including organ transplants and pacemakers—and forgotten factors like clean water and sewage disposal—coupled with a modern determination to stay alive unrivaled in history, mean that in Western society the average person exceeds the biblical three score and ten, an age once considered to be at the upper edge of likelihood. That average increased by an extraordinary twenty years in the course of the second half of the twentieth century.

CHILD mortality strongly affects age averages. In Elizabethan England 2% of babies died before the end of their first day, 5% within a week, 9% in a month and 12–17% in a year. A quarter were dead by the age of five—and that hadn't changed by Victorian times. In fact, in the nineteenth century's industrialized cities, 57 out of every 100 children in working-class families were dead at five. The "world of lost boys" in J. M. Barrie's *Peter Pan* was a metaphor for all such children.

Prehistoric humankind might have settled for a life-span of just the increase—they averaged 18. Ancient Romans averaged 22. During the Elizabethan age expectancy was about 38—Shakespeare didn't do too badly by reaching 52 (dying on his birthday like Plato). That mightn't even warrant a "welcome to middle age" banner at the birthday bash now. In fact, reaching 100 isn't regarded as the phenomenon it once was: several hundred people reach the mark every month, and in Britain the queen doesn't even send centenarians a card anymore. In 1998 there were 135,000 centenari-

 THE Japanese Okinawa islanders are thought to have the highest life expectancy in the world, and the longest health expectancy too, not only aging slowly but escaping dementia, cardiovascular disease, and cancer. There are 457 centenarians on Okinawa—34.7 for every 100,000 inhabitants, compared with fewer than 10 per 100,000 in Britain. The secret, scientists believe, is the combination of lifestyle, a high consumption of grains, vegetables, and fish, a lot of physical activity—and heredity.

An Okinawan saying goes: "At seventy you are still a child, at eighty a young man or woman. And if at ninety someone from heaven invites you over, tell him: 'Just go away and come back when I am a hundred.' "

ans worldwide; by 2050 the projection is 2.2 million—one in every five thousand. Nine in ten will be female.

 ## How Will It Happen?

What makes us die? Lack of breath, children chant, and that's right enough. More specifically, every man, woman, and child dies of the same cause—hypoxemia, a general term for inadequate oxygenation of the blood and cellular tissue. This, we can hope, will be induced by natural causes (in old, old age), but we may be done in by natural disasters, disease, murder, execution, accident, or war. For most of history the Four Horsemen of the Apocalypse—war and strife, famine and pestilence—have seen off men, women, and children by the millions. Now famine and pestilence have been consigned to mythology and the Third World; humankind, however, still seems wholehearted about eliminating other segments of humankind through war and strife.

THE bachelor life may sound tempting to some men, but it doesn't do their health any favors. Research published by the Office of National Statistics in September 2001 revealed that men who live alone after the age of 45 are 50% more likely to die prematurely.

IF you want to "die" without dying—and don't want to go to the trouble of faking it by leaving your clothes on the seashore as British government minister John Stonehouse did in 1974—go to Haiti. There, for a price, you can get a death certificate, no questions asked, complete with video footage of your funeral (close-ups in your coffin) for the benefit of your insurance company. With luck, if you're not caught, you can enjoy the "afterlife" on the insurance payout.

Most other ways of ushering others, or ourselves, to the exit sign are also man-made—a pejorative term, agreed, but testosterone is mostly to blame, and stupidity, which frequently is the same thing.

Surprisingly, considering that life's path is littered with lethal banana skins, over 90 percent of us can expect to die in bed. Now that death is mostly the prerogative of the old—death was less discriminating before the last fifty years or so—almost three-quarters of life's endgames are anticipated and managed. If you want to behave badly and then repent toward the end of the line, the odds are with you. If you're too insecure for that, the best advice is to lead an exemplary existence, as if every day were your last, though the danger is you'll constantly have relatives at your bedside and a priest warming up in the hall. On the other hand, death may come unexpectedly as you go about your business, the heart attack a terrible surprise. *Me? Surely not me. Not yet. There are so many things I want to do. Not yet, please.*

Of course it might just be indigestion.

 ## Done to Death

Wars military, civil, and religious have been history's theoretically avoidable methods of population control. In the main, blame madmen and bad men, and dictators who are likely to be one or both. Napoleon was responsible for the death in battle of half a million Frenchmen, almost a sixth of the French population, for no better reason, when it comes down to it, than his own sense of destiny.

Across the ages the war-religion nexus has always produced a manly brew of violence, from the Christian Crusades against the Muslim powers to take possession of the Holy City of Jerusalem—two hundred years of inglorious glory for God—to the holy wars of the Reformation and Counter-Reformation and the religiously motivated "ethnic cleansing" of European Muslims only a few years ago in the former Yugoslavia. Greed, exploitation, and power are never far behind religious conviction, as amply demonstrated by Pizarro and his conquistadores. If there were available footage, it would show Pizarro's priests marching into Inca townships ahead of the troops, intoning from their Bibles, and exhorting their listeners to reject their gods for the one true faith before sanctioning their deaths; the Incas' incomprehension of Spanish or Latin was taken as a rejection of Christianity.

Religion never did need war to produce bloodshed and death: human sacrifice was part of the history of nearly every form of religion, none more enthusiastic than that of the Aztecs, who honored their gods (and, they thought, nourished the sun) not only with the lives of their enemies but with about a fifth of their own pop-

IN all, 50 million people died in the two world wars. In the second the USSR lost 11 million soldiers—4 out of 5 Russian men born in 1923 were killed. 6 million Jews were murdered by the Nazis, and Stalinist genocide wiped out 60 million people. In the 1970s Pol Pot's Cambodian Khmer Rouge killed between 3 and 4 million. Between 1990 and 2000 civil wars accounted for another 5 million—up to a million minority Tutsi at the hands of the Hutu majority in Rwanda, though in Iraq, Saddam Hussein (against the Kurds), and the Serbian leadership gang in Croatia and Bosnia (against the Croats) and Kosovo (against the Albanians), made significant contributions.

ulation. Preliterate and ancient societies were all prone to eliminating a few people to ensure a good crop.

Human sacrifice as a means of protecting buildings has also had a long history. The ancient Japanese made "human pillars" with even more frequency than gangland Britain in the 1950s put bodies into the foundations of the emerging motorways. One Ashanti king killed two hundred young women and had their blood mixed into the construction of his palace. In that curious blend of Christianity and pagan superstition that characterized medieval Europe, they weren't averse to pushing the odd individual off the top of a new church to sanctify the premises—primitive home insurance for God's house. The Vikings launched new boats over their captives as a tribute to Odin, though being Vikings, they probably did it for the hell of it, too.

 ## Heretics, Deviants, Witches

Medieval Europe kept a sharp eye out for heretics and was ready to dispatch them for the good of their soul. This zeal reached startling heights in the fifteenth century with the Spanish Inquisition. The grand inquisitor Torquemada burned two thousand or so at the stake—an end that may have even been welcome, considering the torture inflicted on them to extract confession of their guilt. Heretic burning became rife across Europe, and Protestants burned heretics with the same conviction as Catholics. Nowhere were people more committed than in England. Despite his break with Rome, Henry VIII roasted heretics with relish. Poor William Tyndale went to the stake for the crime of producing a Bible in contemporary English. Succeeding to her father's throne in 1553, Queen Mary, determined to reconcile England to the Holy See, executed heretics as a solemn religious duty and dispatched more than three hundred before her own demise five years later. Weavers and theologians, upholsterers and village idiots, school boys and the archbishop of Canterbury (Thomas Cranmer) were all tinders to her flames. The lucky ones were sometimes allowed (for suitable recompense) to hang little bags of gunpowder on their legs or around their necks.

The fifteenth, sixteenth, and seventeenth centuries were just as keen on rooting out any deviancy that offended against God's natural order. The philosopher Giordano Bruno went to the stake for dabbling in astrology and alchemy and for supporting Copernicus's theory that the earth revolved around the sun rather than the other way—deviancy indeed, suggesting that man, made by God in his image, was not, after all, the center of the universe. Witchcraft became a heresy in 1563, but those accused of it had long since been hanged, subjected to the lose-lose sink-or-swim test, or burned. For thirty years from 1590 Europe was positively hysterical about witches; so many hapless women were burned—half of them in Germany—that this period was referred to as the Burning Years. A figure of nine million is sometimes suggested for those who died; more sober estimates put it at between sixty and three hundred thousand. In any case, for a further three hundred or so years it was very unfortunate for a woman who was no longer young to live by herself and have a hairy lip. And it was a very bad idea to keep a cat.

THE pope issued a decree in 1484 denouncing all cats. Any woman burned as a witch was to have her cat burned with her. It became customary during Lent to throw cats onto bonfires. Women who killed their husbands were usually hanged but sometimes went to the stake, though as an act of compassion they were usually covered from head to foot in tar to speed the process. Interest in witches waned in the "Age of Reason" of the eighteenth century—but the last "witch" was burned in 1821 for allegedly having sex with the devil and producing eggs that prophesied the future.

Man's (Ingenious) Inhumanity to Man

There's been almost no end to man's (again, let's be pejorative) ingenuity in putting his fellow creatures to death. Variously he has stoned them to death (very popular in biblical times and still today in countries that seem in that time warp), plunged them in boiling oil, skinned them alive, crucified them, roasted them on iron beds over fires, pulled them apart with horses, cut off their heads, hanged, drawn and quartered them, sawed them in half, and broken them with the wheel. And more. There's a satisfaction for history when the biter's bit: Robespierre, architect of the French Reign of Terror, went to the same guillotine that ended fourteen hundred aristos' interest in fashion.

Hanging was and still is the most common means of state execution. In Europe the traditional method suspends the condemned from the gallows or cross-beam until they die of asphyxiation. The "English drop" method, also adopted elsewhere, stands the condemned on a trapdoor; the fall and jerk break the cervical vertebrae. Hanging was preeminent in the United States until the mid-twentieth century. The gas chamber was introduced in the 1920s as being more humane than the electric chair, but many states were reluctant to pull the plug on "Old Sparky," the last two only doing so in

WAS flaying alive, a common execution method around the world, more or less ghastly than the Viking method of cutting open a man's back and bending back his ribs so that he looked like a gull-winged car? Or the Chinese *ling-chy*, "death by the thousand cuts"?

What might have been the cruelest form of execution has been much debated. If the wood was green and too tightly packed to ignite well, those burned at the stake could still be alive as they dropped into the flames, their lower limbs consumed. The man hanged, drawn and quartered—first hanged, then sliced open to have his entrails thrown on a fire—could smell them burning before his heart was plucked out and he lost interest in the proceedings.

And what of the head crusher versus the Iron Maiden, both employed in the Middle Ages? In the former, the victim's chin was placed on a bar, and an iron cap was forced down by a screw, smashing the teeth into their sockets, splintering the facial bones, forcing the eyes from their sockets, and finally squirting the brain through the fragments of the skull. In the latter the victim was put inside a container that had spikes that, when the doors were shut, penetrated his eyes, arms and legs, belly and buttocks, chest and bladder, and the root of his member—though not enough to kill him; it sometimes took two days to die.

After hanging, breaking with the wheel was the most common means of execution throughout Germanic Europe (Gaelic and Latin Europe had something similar employing massive iron bars). The naked victim was stretched on the ground or on a frame with limbs spread and tied to stakes or rings. Wooden cross-beams were placed under the joints, which the executioner then pulped, one by one, with the rim of the huge wheel—wrists, elbows, ankles, knees, hips, shoulders. According to a seventeenth-century chronicler, the victim became "a screaming puppet writhing in rivulets of blood, a puppet with four tentacles, like a sea monster, of raw, slimy and shapeless flesh." Still alive, he was then "plaited" to the wheel's spokes and raised into the air for the crows.

Very possibly the worst death was inflicted with the saw—a method dating back to biblical times and used as late as the Peninsular campaigns (1808–14) of Napoleon and Wellington by Catalonian guerrillas on captured French, British, and Spanish officers. The sawing was conducted not side to side but from the crotch upward. Because the victim was inverted, the brain was amply oxygenated, and the loss of blood minimized. Unconsciousness didn't occur until the saw reached the navel or even the breast.

2002. Essentially, the two thousand volts Old Sparky delivered to the condemned's head depolarized or scrambled the brain signals but also cooked the internal organs: flames were sometimes seen to arise like a vengeful Paraclete. Many found electrocution, in use for 114 years, not much different from burning people at the stake. Now the lethal jab is America's method of choice. China, Iran, and Saudi Arabia execute many more peo-

DURING the nineteenth century it was suggested that the blade of the guillotine cut through the neck so swiftly that the "life force" continued to flow in the brain. When the murderer Languille was guillotined at 5:30 A.M. on June 28, 1905, a Dr. Breauriux "waited for several seconds. The spasmodic movements ceased. The face relaxed, the lids half-closed on the eyeballs, leaving only the white of the conjunctiva visible. . . . It was then that I called in a strong, sharp voice: 'Languille!' I saw the eyelids slowly lift up, without any spasmodic contractions. . . . Next, Languille's eyes very definitely fixed themselves on mine, and the pupils focused themselves. . . . After several seconds, the eyelids slowly closed again. . . . I called out again and, once more, without any spasm, slowly the eyelids lifted and undeniably living eyes fixed themselves on mine with perhaps even more penetration than the first time." Modern medical opinion is that this and other anecdotes describe only the involuntary twitching of the muscles after death, but the subject was still being debated in 2002 on the *New Scientist* website.

ple than the United States (China over a thousand a year; the U.S. well under a hundred), but seventy-three nations, including all of western Europe, have abolished the death penalty. Britain did so in 1965, in an act unlamented save by a small clique of unreconstituted Tories.

The days of public execution, while available elsewhere, have long been gone in Europe. (The last public

IN the seventeenth century the English public hangman was Derrick, who devised a structure on which twenty-three condemned could be hanged together. The device was later put to use loading and unloading ships—and still bears Derrick's name.

hanging in Britain was in 1868; the last one in America wasn't until 1936.) But what spectacle they provided! Just as in 1555 a triple burning in Dartford attracted such a crowd that farmers sold cartloads of fresh cherries, so in Victorian London a good hanging was street entertainment and good business for those selling pies from trays. Children were hoisted on shoulders for a better look. British novelist Thackeray went to one hanging and noted that the windows of the shops and the balconies were filled with dandies, "quiet, fat, family parties," and rowdy upper classes squirting soda siphons, but at the last minute he was unnerved by the great murmur of the crowd

HANGING offenses in Britain in the nineteenth century included trying to commit suicide, stealing a loaf of bread, setting fire to a haystack, writing a threatening letter, being on the highway with a sooty face, associating with Gypsies, and writing graffiti on Westminster Bridge.

and couldn't look. At another Dickens saw "the image of the Devil" in the "wickedness and levity" of the mob.

We wouldn't have the stomach for the fare of public execution today, would we? But would we watch on television?

 ## Kill Thy Neighbor

When it comes to the major reason for execution—murder—America tends to excel. It isn't at the top of the league, but between 1976 and 1993 more U.S. citizens were murdered than died in the Second World War. Worse, murder is the second leading cause of death among fifteen-to-twenty-four-year-olds, and third among the five-to-fourteen age group. A third of all murders are committed by the first age group, which itself is sixteen times more likely to be murdered than the rest of Americans.

But the title of top kill-thy-neighbor nation, according to the United Nations, belongs to South Africa: 22,000 a

THE world's first murderer was Cain, eldest son of Adam and Eve, who murdered his brother Abel, jealous that his brother's sacrifice was more acceptable to God than his own.

IN the wake of school shootings many schools now rehearse protective strategies, including how to use the desk as a shield.

year, in a population of 40 million. With a population six and a half times greater, the U.S. figure is 20,000—and down by more than 3,000 since 1991. Brazil and little Jamaica (2.5 million, 1,100 murders) follow South Africa. Singapore, known for its zero tolerance policy, is virtually a murder-free zone—3 a year in a population of 3 million or, to put that another way, 0.1 per 100,000 population. Only Britain, Cyprus, and the Slovak Republic, with a rate of 0.5 per 100,000, come even close.

Murder most foul traditionally relied on something blunt and heavy or sharp and pointy but lost ground once gunpowder was invented and small pieces of metal could be projected at great velocity from larger pieces of metal. Yet even where gun deaths are concerned, South Africa, Brazil, and Jamaica are gunshot lengths ahead of the United States: South Africa and Brazil have four

A 1993 U.S. survey of women in the workplace found that more secretaries were murdered on the job than police officers and bartenders combined.

PREPARING a case for trial in 1997 that carried the death penalty, attorney William Linka analyzed hundreds of cases from legal records, noting that 8.3% of those convicted for murder were called Lee; 5.4% were called Dwayne or Duane; 13% had an added "Junior" or "Senior"; and 19.4% had no middle name. 7% of those convicted met two or more of these factors, and 41% one.

times and Jamaica three times as many shootings per capita. The world's only superpower can't head the field in everything. Nonetheless 14,000 of America's 20,000 annual murders are carried out with guns.

 Oops, Accident!

Accidents happen: the wrong place, the wrong time—unavoidable. Call it the Aeschylus syndrome—the Greek dramatist was killed by a tortoise dropped on his bald pate by an eagle. The list of sufferers of this syndrome is long. The Roman emperor Claudius choked to death at a banquet on the feather with which he was tickling his gullet to induce vomiting. The only English pope, Adrian IV, went similarly on an accidentally swallowed fly. The philosopher and proponent of the scientific method, Francis Bacon, caught pneumonia on a freezing day, experimentally stuffing a chicken with snow as an alternative preservative to salt. The French composer Jean Baptiste Lully got so carried away while conducting that he speared his foot with the staff with which he was keeping time and gave himself a fatal dose of blood poisoning. Things change: everything remains the same. In 1998 a seventeen-year-old English lad, so obsessive about personal hygiene that he used can after can of deodorant, died because the propane and butane propellants built up a lethal dosage in his body. The same year a young Saudi who answered a call on his cell phone at the top of a South African mountain was killed when lightning struck the phone. In 2001 a forty-four-year-old Frenchman choked on his girlfriend's edible underwear.

Accidents kill more people than die early in any other way and very possibly always have. The construction worker who falls off his scaffolding is only following some ancient Egyptian who did likewise on the Great Pyramid. The workplace is a dangerous place. Balzac's death has to be called work related: the nineteenth-

NATURAL disasters killed 50,000 people in 1990–2000.

THE bathroom is a dangerous place, not that you can avoid it. The chronically constipated who've died there include Catherine the Great of Russia, Evelyn Waugh, and Elvis Presley—all cases of dying to go and dying while trying. Another was English king George II, whose *valet de chambre* heard a noise from the palace privy that he thought "louder than the usual royal wind" and found the king dead on the floor.

Toilets can be dangerous in other respects. The Saxon king Edmund Ironside was killed by an assassin hiding in the pit beneath his lavatorial throne, who thrust a longsword up the royal back passage.

century novelist died of caffeine poisoning—he drank fifty cups of black coffee a day. Work killed the Italian stripper Gina Lalapola, who in Cosenza in 1997 disappointed a stag party by not leaping out of a giant cake because she'd suffocated. Work itself kills ten thousand Tokyo businessmen every year, thanks to a hundred-hour, seven-day-a-week commitment that involves sleeping in the office on two or three nights and never taking the full annual vacation entitlement. There's even a word for such work-induced checkouts: *koroski*.

Far and away the biggest cause of avoidable death is motor vehicles. Around forty thousand road deaths

IN Washington, D.C., Latino pedestrians are three times more likely than other residents to be killed by a car.

occur in the United States annually, three thousand in the U.K., and some 40 percent are estimated to be drink or drug related—as, collectively, are all kinds of theoretically avoidable exits. Half of all those who kill themselves off in cars—a proportion, in Canada, racing trains to unmanned crossings—are males under the age of twenty-four. This comes as no surprise to anyone except males under the age of twenty-four, who discover too late that being young and male isn't a guarantee of invincibility.

Cause of Death: Stupidity

Stupidity doesn't appear on any death certificate, but perhaps it should. It isn't, of course, the exclusive pre-

THE Darwin Awards were started in 1993 to commemorate the lives of people who did something spectacularly—and terminally—mindless. Read *The Darwin Awards* books or visit www.DarwinAwards.com for tales of men and women "who have improved our gene pool by killing themselves in really stupid ways."

serve of youth: in many people the commonsense gene just doesn't develop, and they remain a screw short of a coffin lid. One such was the would-be robber who in 1990 entered a Washington gun shop, announced a hold-up, and fired off a few shots—this despite a marked police car parked outside the door, a police officer drinking coffee at the counter, and a shop full of customers, in a state where a high proportion of the adult population is licensed to carry handguns. We don't need to ask "What happened next?" Another was the man who electrocuted fish with household current and then waded in to collect his catch without removing the wire; then there was the respiratory patient who lit a cigarette in an oxygen tent; and the terrorist who mailed a letter bomb with insufficient postage, then opened the returned package. What possessed the twenty-four-year-old who in 1982 attempted to cure his severe hemorrhoids with a can of petrol? Fame or position is no defense against terminal stupidity. In the

 TYCHO Brahe, the sixteenth-century Danish astronomer whose research helped Sir Isaac Newton arrive at the theory of gravity, died of politeness. He'd drunk a lot at a banquet and needed to relieve himself but was too self-conscious to leave the table. His bladder burst.

nineteenth century, when a DIY bloodletting kit came on the market, Queen Caroline of Bavaria bought one and mistakenly opened an artery. In 1931 the English novelist Arnold Bennett drank a glass of tap water in a Paris hotel to show that it was free from typhoid. In 1976 The Yardbirds' Keith Relf played his electric guitar in the bathtub. In 1989 the famous Indian mystic Khadeshwari Babi had himself buried in a hole for ten days to show his powers of meditation.

The story that follows is one that's been circulating as fact on the Internet for years, despite being attributed alternately to the fictional *East Arkansas Press* and the genuine but less-than-reliable *Weekly World News*:

"I was slowing down, but Georgann wouldn't wait till I stopped," Everett Williams told police after the death of his wife in a freak motoring accident in Arkansas City. "We both saw Jesus at the side of the road, with what looked like twelve people slowly floating up into the air. She started screaming, 'He's back! Jesus is back!' and we both thought that the rapture was happening. I tried to pull over, but she wouldn't wait, because she was convinced Jesus was going to lift her up into the sky, there and then. Before I could stop, she climbed right out of the

sunroof crying 'Take me Lord!', jumped off the car, and was run over by the car behind."

Officer Paul Madison later explained: "What we have here is a case of mistaken rapture. It seems that a motorist, Ernie Jenkins, was on his way to a toga costume dressed as Jesus, with twelve blow-up sex dolls filled with helium in his truck. The tarp covering the dolls came loose and they started floating into the air, so he stopped, got out, and tried to catch them. The Williamses were driving past, saw Mr. Jenkins with his arms raised high, assumed it was the Second Coming of Jesus, and Mrs. Williams jumped to the wrong conclusion. And to her death."

"People have often told me I look like Jesus," said Jenkins. "That's why I thought I'd go to the party as Christ with his twelve disciples. I wish I'd gone as Nero instead."

Some death can't be neatly classified as dead unlucky or dead stupid—just bizarre. Nothing can top what follows: at the 1994 annual awards dinner for Forensic Science, the president, Dr. Don Harper Mills, astounded his audience with a story (later confessed to have been made up for the purpose of entertaining his fellow forensic scientists) of the death of Ronald Opus on March 23rd that year.

Opus had jumped from the top of a ten-story building. As he fell past the ninth floor, he was killed by a shotgun blast to the head. What Opus didn't know was that farther down a safety net had been put up to protect some building workers, so his suicide bid would have failed. The medical examiner therefore felt he was dealing with a homicide.

The fatal blast had come from an apartment where an elderly man was threatening his wife with a shotgun. Confronted with the murder charge, the old man and his wife were adamant that they thought the shotgun was unloaded. An accident, then.

The continuing investigation turned up a witness who saw the old couple's son loading the shotgun weeks earlier. It transpired that the old lady had cut off her son's financial support, and knowing his father's habit of waving the shotgun around during arguments with his mother, he had loaded the gun in the expectation that his father would shoot his mother.

Opus's death once more appeared to be murder, by the son. But the son was, in fact, Opus. Increasingly despondent over the failure of his plan, Opus had decided on suicide and, in effect, murdered himself.

The medical examiner closed the case as suicide.

Where accidents are concerned, probability experts classify people in response to their attitudes to risk: risk averse, risk neutral, and risk seeking. Most of us are risk neutral in most things we do. If we were risk averse in everything, we wouldn't ride in a car, take a shower, answer the phone, walk the dog—or eat or drink. They can all kill you. If you are entirely risk seeking (back to supercharged testosterone and a philosophy that if you're standing on the edge you're taking up too much room), you stand a good chance of dying young.

 CAN a human suddenly burst into flames for no discernible reason? The first documented case of spontaneous human combustion (SHC) was reported in 1662, and by the time Charles Dickens killed off the villainous Krook in *Bleak House* in this manner there were over thirty.

In the nineteenth century it was believed that heavy drinking produced an accumulation of combustible substances in the body that could be ignited by a spark of the body's own electricity. The more rational explanation is that a victim had been close to a source of fire. Once clothing is alight, it burns the skin and then melts the subcutaneous fat, which soaks into the clothing, making it into a wick—which explains why parts of a body that are uncovered don't burn. Over three-quarters of SHCs are women who are overweight (and have copious fat), sedentary—and heavy drinkers.

Problem: in some cases of SHC there has been no fire source . . .

Odds Against Death by Mishap

In the wake of September 11, the likelihood of dying in a hijacked and crashed airliner exercised the number crunchers. They concluded that if you fly once a year, the odds are six million to one. If terrorists crash a single plane a year, the odds become 72 million to one. In fact, you're 1,350 times more likely to die of a heart attack than a terrorist hijacking, which should make you feel better—unless you are particularly worried about dying of a heart attack.

The odds against you being murdered depends on your country of residence, your neighborhood, who you hang out with, and your gender and age (let's not go there again). Broadly, the odds against it happening to any American are 13,000 to 1; 60,000 to 1 for a British citizen; and 2,000 to 1 for a South African.

ACTUARIAL odds against some means of accidental death in a single year—and over a lifetime, for pessimists: car crash (6,000–1, 80–1); walking (44,000–1, 600–1); air crash (250,000–1, 3,000–1); falling object (360,000–1, 5,000–1); rail crash (470,000–1, 7,000–1); lightning (4,200,000–1, 55,000–1); hornets, wasps, bees (5,800,000–1, 270,000–1); dog bite (11,500,000–1, 150,000–1); fireworks (30,000,000–1, 390,000–1).

IN 1989 an experiment was carried out with twenty-two American municipal judges. Half were asked to write about their own death, what physically happens, and what emotions thinking about death evoked. When asked to set bail for a prostitute on the basis of a case brief, these eleven judges set an average of $455. The other eleven—who hadn't addressed their own death—set an average of $50. The authors' conclusion: when awareness of death is increased, prejudice against other groups and religious extremism escalate.

 ## Suicide: The Self-Destruct Button

Suicide is usually a game of solitaire, except among the old who have been married a long time, and infrequently, the young. The writer Arthur Koestler and his wife agreed to go together in 1977; during the last decade there have been several "sophomore suicides" in the United States among female teenagers; in 2000 three teenage boys in Berlin who'd taken to devil worship daubed their bodies with pentacles and leapt from a bridge.

Mass suicide is even rarer. Most famously in ancient history, 960 Jewish Zealots, no longer able to hold out against the Romans in the stronghold of Masada, agreed to die together rather than surrender. In modern times a combination of extreme religious conviction

and apocalyptic prophecy from the mouth of charis-
matic charlatans has led to all-together death pacts. In
1978, 913 members of James Warren Jones's People's
Temple in the colony of Jonestown, in a Guyanan rain
forest, committed "revolutionary suicide" with him,
drinking cyanide. (Jones, who said he was the reincarnation of both Jesus and Lenin, shot himself.) In March
2000 in Uganda 235 members of the Movement for the
Restoration of the Ten Commandments of God allowed
themselves to be locked in a church that was then
burned down—they believed the world was about to
end, on the word of the movement's founder, a prosti-
tute-turned-medium who was tipped off by the Virgin
Mary. During the 1990s seventy-four members of the
Order of the Solar Temple—which believed that death
by fire led to rebirth on the star Sirius—went on "death
voyages" in various locations in Europe and Canada.
But the temple's activities were overshadowed by another doomsday sect with a space fixation—Maurice
Applewhite's Heaven's Gate. Convinced in 1997 that
the Hale-Bopp comet trailed behind it a UFO four times
the size of earth, the former California music teacher
convinced his congregation to shed their "earthly con-
tainers" by drinking apple juice and vodka laced with
pentobarbital after a last supper, then waiting for Scotty

KING Mithridates VI, who ruled in Asia Minor in the first century B.C., took small doses of poison to build up resistance in case anyone tried to kill him. When he was about to fall into the hands of the Romans, he tried a hasty exit—with poison. It didn't work. A slave had to finish the job with a sword. The term *mithridate* means "antidote."

to beam them up. The local sheriff found thirty-nine bodies, each with an overnight bag and the sum of five dollars, presumably to pay the space ferryman.

Attitudes to suicide have varied in history. In ancient Greece convicted criminals were allowed to take their own life; in Ceo it was obligatory for all people over sixty. Imperial Rome considered suicide honorable. Judaic, Christian, and Islamic law all declared against it, and in many European countries—where the word was unknown before the middle of the seventeenth century—the body of a suicide was officially mutilated and their property seized. In France attempted suicide was no longer illegal after the Revolution, and most of Europe gradually followed suit. England hanged failed suicides until the nineteenth century, and suicide didn't cease to be a crime until 1961.

The East has generally had a more sympathetic atti-

INTENT on ending his own life, the mad Roman emperor Heliogabalus armed himself with a golden sword, a priceless ring containing poison, and a rope of imperial purple and gold. Unsure how the mood might take him, he also ordered a patio of jewels beneath one of his towers. The best laid plans . . . He was run through by one of his guards.

tude. Christianity denied those who had taken their life burial rites and internment in hallowed ground. Muslims, like the ancient Egyptians, have always buried them like anyone else and don't see suicide as a bar to the afterlife. Nor do Hindus, though suicides, like murderers, aren't cremated—their spirits are considered too angry to be ritually purified, and instead they're buried or thrown in the river.

The most common means of achieving self-termination down the ages have been by drowning, jumping, hanging, or throat-cutting. The Romans favored hemlock or slitting the wrists in the bath, though falling on your sword was frequent in a tight spot. Among the samurai in Japan *seppuku* (self-disembowelment)—which we mistakenly call "hara-kiri"—was no less honorable in defeat and obligatory for warriors found guilty of a crime. Once firearms became widely available everywhere, shooting, naturally enough, offered attractions, as did coal gas on its introduction. (Natural gas, which replaced it, is no good for the task.) Today most female suicides choose drugs, often saved up from prescriptions. Man's love affair with the car means that most male suicides prefer a dose of carbon monoxide hosed from their exhaust. Self-immolation, practiced by Buddhist monks and Asian students in protest against social and legal conditions, is very much a minority option.

The old ways, of course, never go out of fashion, especially jumping. But tall buildings, while they serve the purpose, aren't as alluring as high places near or over water. From its construction in the 1930s San Francisco's Golden Gate Bridge was the brand name—a tally of more than six hundred suicides; but in recent years Beachy Head, where Sussex meets the English Channel, has become a prime spot, with around twenty a year taking the seven-second plunge down the 535-foot drop. On four separate occasions three people have gone over on the same day.

In the West the suicide rate has fallen by a fifth in the last forty years, but in the last twenty it has increased dramatically among adolescents across the world. Young male suicides have tripled. In the United States suicide is the third leading cause of all teenage deaths—one every two hours.

SEPPUKU was abolished by law in 1873 but still appeals to the Japanese mind. The novelist Yukio Mishima employed it in 1970 after delivering his final manuscript. With several followers he seized control of a Tokyo military HQ in a protest against the postwar constitution forbidding war and rearmament and urged the army to overthrow the government. His response was to their lack of one.

Greenland has the highest per capita suicide rate, with 127 per 100,000 population; Hungary has 37, Finland 27.8, Austria 20.6, Switzerland 19.1, France 18.9, Sweden and Norway 16, Germany 15.5, the United States 12.3, Scotland 10.8, and England and Wales 7.4. China, home to 21 percent of all the women in the world, accounts for over half of all female sui-

BEFORE the events of September 11, 2001, the Japanese kamikaze pilots of the Second World War had been alone in using aircraft as flying bombs. Their suicide missions sank thirty-four ships in the U.S. fleet, damaged hundreds of others, and at Okinawa killed almost five thousand men. *Kamikaze* means "divine wind," a reference to a typhoon that scattered an invading Mongol fleet in the thirteenth century.

THE saddest suicide in fiction is that of the three children in Thomas Hardy's *Jude the Obscure* who hanged themselves on hooks behind the door—done, as Jude's son little Jude wrote on a piece of paper, "because we are too menny."

cides; peasant girls married off or even sold to older, abusive husbands to do most of the work on the farms prefer swallowing pesticides.

The reasons people turn to the last page without letting the tale unfold are legion: illness, depression, unrequited love, boredom, self-pity, voices in the head—even imitation. Los Angeles experienced a 40 percent increase

THE Complete Manual of Suicide became a runaway Japanese best seller in 1999. The manual promised readers "the peace of mind of knowing you can leave this troubled world whenever you choose." It detailed ten methods, including hanging, electrocution, and immolation, and compared them in terms of quickness and disfigurement. Illustrated with charts, maps, and *manga* drawings, it made recommendations about the best spots to die, gave tips about avoiding detection, and described celebrity suicides. The book has been blamed for the rising body count in Aokigahara, a dense wood at the foot of Mount Fuji that is described as "the perfect place." 74 corpses have turned up there.

THE local magistrate in ancient Athens kept a supply of hemlock for the elderly, depressed, or terminally ill. Scandinavian and Eskimo cultures traditionally left the old or infirm in the snow to let nature take its course. The South African Hottentots put on a big bash before abandoning someone in the wilderness.

Quietly, doctors have always helped the terminally ill end their pain, but the matter has come into the open in the last twenty-five years. In the Netherlands in 1994 it was calculated there were 2,300 cases of euthanasia and 400 of assisted suicide. The behavior of the retired pathologist Jack Kevorkian, who made machines that allowed people to kill themselves, largely turned public opinion against the concept of hastening death actively, but passive assistance—the withdrawing of life-sustaining treatment—is acceptable to most people.

in 1962 after Marilyn Monroe's last encounter with her sleeping pills, which was as nothing compared with what happened in Japan in the 1930s, when over a two-year period 1,207 people copied a schoolgirl who'd jumped into the crater of a volcano on the island of Oshima. The authorities dealt with the situation by forbidding the sale of one-way tickets on the ferries going there.

Whatever the reasons, they can be summed up in a word: *unhappiness,* unhappiness that is all consuming. For the vast majority of us it never gets that bad, however bad it gets. "The advocates for suicide tell us that it's quite permissible to quit our house when we are weary of it," Voltaire wrote. "Agreed—but most men would rather live in a ramshackle house than sleep in the open fields."

 ## Microbes: Natural-Born Killers

Now as always, disease causes most of the deaths that, by and large, we have to regard as unavoidable. But more than four million people worldwide die every year from avoidable tobacco-related illnesses. (That's not entirely true: around thirty thousand are innocent bystanders— passive smokers.) The biggest killer in the Western world, heart disease, carries off eight times as many people as accidents, and cancer, the second-biggest killer, accounts for nearly six times. With every drag of a cigarette a smoker inhales 4,700 different chemicals, including ammonia, arsenic, and cyanide. And they're surprised that on average they lose twelve years of their lives? Like stupidity, smoking doesn't appear on a death certificate, yet one way or another the habit kills a third of addicts; according to the latest figures it will eventually send half of all under-twenties in China, the leading consumer of cigarettes (31 percent), into their graves.

Perhaps smoking should be redesignated as suicide in slow motion.

DYING is good for . . . the state. A report for the Czech government in 2001 concluded that smokers saved the state millions by dying prematurely.

Until the last century communicable diseases were the main causes of death: plague, typhus, smallpox, cholera, tuberculosis, diphtheria, scarlet fever, whooping cough, measles, influenza. Collectively they felled a quarter of populations. The plague or Black Death of the fourteenth century was the most virulent and devastating pandemic in human history—between a third and a half of those living in northern Africa, Europe, and Asia from China to Greenland perished. In Europe alone twenty million died. "In men and women alike," commented Boccaccio on the devastation in Florence, "it first betrayed itself by the emergency of certain tumours in the groin or the armpits, some of which grew as large as a common apple, others as an egg." An English chronicler wrote with disgust that "all the matter which exudes from their bodies let off an unbearable stench." The plague was almost always fatal. Ashes, ashes, we all fall down. The Spanish flu pandemic that swept the globe in 1918–19 carried off thirty million, albeit from a much greater population base. It took twenty-five million in the first six months. During the last year of the First World War, 34,000 American soldiers died in battle; 24,000 died of flu.

Since the 1930s protective vaccines, antibiotics, and other antimicrobial drugs have changed the situation, but microbes, viruses, bacteria, and other smaller groups of organisms are never beaten, just kept at bay. They have an advantage: they replicate by division, not sex, and they operate inside a safe and ideal environment—us. They develop immunity, too, and new strains. Increasing international travel makes them globetrotters, though there's nothing new in that. Columbus's reaching the New World forged contact between two human populations that had been isolated from each other for thousands of years and unleashed the worst health disaster there's ever been. Waves of European communicable diseases

WORLDWIDE 22 million people have died of AIDS, and 36 million are infected by the human immunodeficiency virus. Hardest hit is Botswana, where AIDS is responsible for one in four deaths. In 1999 250,000 to 300,000 South Africans died of it—40% of all deaths in the 15–49 age group, and this number is expected to treble by 2007. President Mbeki says HIV is not the cause, and his government has declared a World Health Organization report to be "not credible." But the government has sponsored two "cures": an industrial solvent and a treatment made from burnt coal.

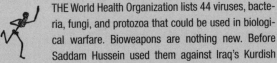

THE World Health Organization lists 44 viruses, bacteria, fungi, and protozoa that could be used in biological warfare. Bioweapons are nothing new. Before Saddam Hussein used them against Iraq's Kurdish minority during the Iran-Iraq War, the Assyrians catapulted rotting animal carcasses over the wall of cities they besieged to spread disease; the Romans tossed corpses into their enemies' water supplies; and in the eighteenth century British soldiers deliberately distributed smallpox-infected blankets to American Indians.

wiped out swaths of native peoples whose immune systems couldn't cope.

Arguably the New World got its own back. It's thought that Columbus's men imported a killer disease in exchange for their exports: syphilis.

Drugs preventive and curative have staved off death for humankind, but they have also introduced it. Many people are such ardent poppers of over-the-counter pills and potions that they cause their own demise. But overprescription of drugs by doctors and wrong administration of them in hospitals are a bigger danger—and when deaths from infections picked up in hospitals and preventable medical errors are added together, the figures are staggering. It's a world phenomenon. In the United States medical drugs are the third-biggest killer, after heart disease and cancer. In Britain in 2001 hospital infections killed sixteen thousand. In the past decade it's estimated that Western medical practice has unnecessarily done in five million people.

Until little over a hundred years ago, doctors had an even worse track record: they killed almost as many as they cured. "You medical people will have more lives to answer for in the other world than even we generals," Napoleon said.

The most dangerous doctor of all time was the second-century anatomist Galen, personal physician to the Roman emperor Marcus Aurelius. Quite possibly he's helped kill more people than any medical man in history, which is saying something. According to Galen, the brain was a clot of phlegm, the heart had two chambers, the cure for a headache was to cut holes in the skull, and the cure for a cough was to remove the uvula—not unreasonable conclusions from someone

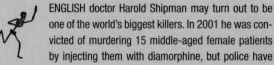

ENGLISH doctor Harold Shipman may turn out to be one of the world's biggest killers. In 2001 he was convicted of murdering 15 middle-aged female patients by injecting them with diamorphine, but police have evidence in 25 other cases and believe his tally could be 150. In his 24-year career Shipman recorded 297 more deaths than any other doctor in the area over the same period.

whose medical knowledge was gained from studying dead pigs and dogs and by guesswork. Yet for more than a thousand years Galen stood as the medical authority, and the Church made it a heresy to question him. Held back by this and unable to familiarize themselves with human plumbing because of the Church's ban on anatomical dissection, doctors undoubtedly did their best. But ignorance was bliss. A medieval pope died after an infusion of a younger person's more vibrant blood. Blood types? What are blood types? In 1667 Samuel Pepys watched a clergyman be given a transfusion of sheep's blood before members of the Royal Society and noted in his diary that before the clergyman died he appeared "cracked a little in his head."

The purges, emetics, and prolonged bleeding favored in the seventeenth and eighteenth centuries hastened the majority of those thus treated into the

PUERPERAL fever—childbed fever—killed Jane Seymour, Henry VIII's third wife, and an estimated 1 in 7 new mothers throughout history—1 in 5 during the worst epidemics of seventeenth- and eighteenth-century Europe. In the early 1900s 3,000 women died in childbirth every year—5 mothers for every one 1,000 births. In 1992, out of 4 million births in the U.S., only 302 mothers died from all birth-related causes.

afterlife, including King Charles II. The resident physician at Versailles similarly treated the French royal family for measles and did in the lot, including Louis XIV (the infant and future Louis XV was saved by the nurses who hid him), earning himself the sobriquet the "killer of princes." Ignorant of germs, surgeons wiped their bloody hands on their frock coats and cut up corpses in front of crowds, often with a fire in the room and dogs sleeping on the floor. Germ theory was derided by some even after the discoveries of Joseph Lister, the father of antiseptic surgery, and as late as the mid-nineteenth century women were dying of puerperal fever because doctors used unsterilized instruments and they and midwives moved from patient to patient frequently without washing their hands.

Trust me, I'm a doctor. Yeah?

 ## Death and the "Little Death"

The Oxford English Dictionary connects *orgasm* with *rage,* but some language scholars maintain that the Old English root is the same as for *death.* Intercourse can make you feel as though you've temporarily expired, which is why the French dub orgasm *la petite mort*—"the little death."

As has often been pointed out, there's a deeply ambiguous link between sex and religion. You recover from *la petite mort* and carry on happily in life; you don't recover from *la grande mort,* but religion hopes that you carry on happily in the afterlife. Psychiatry argues that sexual taboos, institutionalized through religion, are a disguised attempt to keep death away. Sometimes the link between sex and religion, as in the matter of religious ecstasy, is, as Steve Jones's *In the Blood* points out, "embarrassingly clear":

> *St. Teresa of Avila had a vision of Christ. "In his hands I saw a long golden spear . . . he seemed to pierce my heart several times so that it penetrated to my entrails. When he drew it out . . . he left me afire with a continual love of God."*

That's what too much fasting does for you.

In the Middle Ages Catholics who were thought to be at death's door received the last rites, as they do now. If, however, they recovered, they were thereafter forbidden to have sex. Make of that what you will. Like the ancient Chinese, the Victorians widely believed that a man's sexual activity shortened his life span—each orgasm "spent" finite reserves and brought him closer to death. They couldn't have been more wrong, according to much modern research. A ten-year study of middle-aged and older males in the Welsh town of

Caerphilly found that those who reported the most frequent orgasms—a hundred a year—had less than half the risk of death as other men of their age, particularly from coronary heart disease.

Other research shows that the benefits of intercourse go into reverse if the male's sexual partner isn't his long-term one. In the early 1960s a young woman pushed a pram into a south London police station. In it was the body of her middle-aged lover who'd died *in flagrante delicto.* The woman had brought him to the cop shop because she didn't want him at home when her husband got back. Despite being generally beneficial, sexual exertion has undoubtedly killed many less-than-young men. In a long list of the famous we have the fifth-century barbarian Attila, who burst an artery on his wedding night with his twelfth wife; British prime minister Lord Palmerston, snookered on his billiard table with a young parlormaid (1865); French president

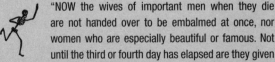

"NOW the wives of important men when they die are not handed over to be embalmed at once, nor women who are especially beautiful or famous. Not until the third or fourth day has elapsed are they given to the embalmers. They do this to prevent the embalmers violating the corpse."   —Herodotus

Félix Faure in a Parisian brothel (1899); and a former U.S. vice president Nelson Rockefeller, in the arms of his mistress (1975). The prodigious Errol Flynn checked out as he had lived, a swordsman to the last.

 ## How Do You Know You're Dead?

Children find it hard to understand death. In *The Interpretation of Dreams* Freud wrote a footnote about a highly intelligent boy of ten who remarked after the sudden death of his father: "I know father's dead, but what I can't understand is why he doesn't come home to supper." Even adults find it hard to imagine themselves dead. As a character in Tom Stoppard's play *Rosencrantz and Guildenstern Are Dead* asks: "Do you ever think of yourself as actually dead, lying in a box with a lid on it? . . . I mean, think of it like being alive in a box." When the American writer William Saroyan telephoned the Associated Press shortly before his death in 1981, he was only half joking when he observed: "Everybody has got to die, but I have always believed an exception would be made in my case. Now what?"

Once, death was a simple matter: you were alive or you weren't. There were several tests, if necessary: freezing water poured in the ear (involuntary reflex); a poke in the eye (corneal reflex); something stuck down the throat

IN his memoirs Alexandre Dumas related how, on hearing of the death of his father, he got a gun and went upstairs, telling his mother that he was going to the sky, "because that was where God lived and I was going to kill God, who killed Father."

(gag reflex); knuckles ground in the sternum (pain reflex). In imperial Rome when a man breathed his last, his name was cried aloud; if he didn't reply, he was dead. Zoroastrians believe that a dog with eye-shaped spots on its forehead will give a sure sign: if it shows no interest when brought into the room where death has probably occurred, you can forget the "probably"; if it does show interest, any of the above-mentioned tests may be apt.

But advances in medical technology, and ethics, have complicated the issue. As someone remarked, you can only really be sure a person is dead if they're no longer capable of litigation. Lack of detectable respiration and heartbeat are no longer seen as absolutes, and even electroencephalographic measurement of the activity of the brain—which can remain alive for up to ten minutes after the heart has stopped—can't be relied on entirely. The literature is full of cases of people "dying," having no response to stimuli, no EEG measure, and yet being resuscitated.

Once a person knows they're dying, according to the psychiatrist Elisabeth Kübler-Ross, they typically go through five stages: denial; anger; "bargaining" for more time; depression; and lastly acceptance. It's a way of handling their dying—though bypassed if run over by the hypothetical No. 7 bus or similar. The Hindu alternative is to view life as the illusion and death as the real thing.

When someone dies, sight is the first of the senses to go, followed by taste, smell, touch, and finally hearing. According to Tibetan Buddhist belief, the mind and the body's energies withdraw and begin to dissolve into each other. The earth energy dissolves into the water energy, and a feeling of weakness accompanies the loss of sight. As the hearing is lost, the dying person feels as if they're drying out and surrounded by smoke. Finally they're adrift in a sky of moonlight, then sunlight, then darkness, the point of death, at which time the pilgrimage toward rebirth begins.

You're unaware of the moment you stepped over the

 MEDIEVAL Japan believed that there was a single hair somewhere on the tail of a cat that could restore life to the dying. As a last hope, a cat was brought into the room for the dying person to try his or her luck.

threshold into life. With luck you won't be aware you're going in the opposite direction. If your religious conviction is justified, you'll know you've departed this life; if not, you won't. Either way, as a Kingsley Amis poem notes, there's something to be said for death: "Wherever you may be / They bring it to you, free."

DEAD NERVOUS (or) NERVOUS OF THE DEAD

 Precautions Against Death

The attitude of the living towards the dead has always been ambivalent. Throughout time the living have done everything to maintain their links with the dead, but also to sever them. The respect shown to the dead—the rituals observed, the stocking of the grave—was to ensure their safe passage to the hereafter but had every bit as much to do with self-protection. If the dead were dissatisfied with their treatment then, like the traditional mother-in-law, they might come back. And back.

Many of the observations of death that we consider simply as marks of respect once had undertows. The eyes of the just-departed were closed to ensure that someone didn't accidentally look into them and see their own demise. Eyes were often not simply closed or covered: they were plugged with wax or pinned tight— the dead went onward with their eyes wide shut. In medieval Europe mirrors were turned to the wall and standing water thrown out for the same reasons, though standing water was often sprinkled or brought back into the house after the corpse was gone—in virtually all cultures the dead were thought to travel over water to their destination but were unable to come back over it. In Hindu rites today, water is poured across the path as mourners leave the graveside to prevent the soul from following.

A corpse was seen as a potential source of peril. In parts of Africa still, children and pregnant women aren't allowed to look, and in China at the moment that a diviner calculates the soul will leave, everyone quits the room because of the possible danger. Swift burial in Judaism and Zoroastrianism, and cremation in Hinduism, were originally to get the dead safely away to prevent death, like a contagion, from polluting the place of its occurrence and those associated with it. In many cultures circles were or are drawn around a corpse to stop the "pollution" from escaping, a fear that led to the observation of a mourning period to "disinfect" the relatives while

ANTHROPOLOGICAL evidence suggests that primitive white men painted their bodies black at funerals to disguise themselves from spirits; black African tribes coat their bodies the opposite color for the same reason.

ensuring that the wider community remained uncontaminated. The shovel used to sprinkle soil onto a coffin at a Jewish funeral is laid down, not passed from person to person—a token recognition of the contagion of death.

In handling the dead, every culture has deemed it wise to tread carefully. The vigil over the body might have been partly to ensure it showed no twitch of life, but it was more to do with guarding against the soul reentering or some wandering spirit breaking in to squat— which is why the openings of the body were invariably stopped up. In parts of Africa today oil or butter is used for the purpose, and the eyes and mouth are bound with strips of cloth. In a region of Romania the bereaved don't cry but dance and sing, so that any evil spirits will think there's a party going on, not a fresh corpse up for grabs. In many native societies the belief that the dead may try to return and will come back the way they left has led to the practice of taking a body out of the domicile through the window or a hole made in the wall or tent. The name of the game has been confusion.

The Greeks and Romans buried their dead outside the city primarily for sanitary reasons, but putting a bit of distance between them and the living was a precaution, too, and early Roman burials were carried out at night as another disorienting tactic. Greeks, Romans, Europeans, Japanese, and American colonists all favored crossroads as spots of ultimate confusion, utilized for burying executed criminals and suicides, murderers and the victims of murder—all those who might hold a grudge and be particularly likely to go about seeking retribution. The accumulation of such burials made crossroads dangerous places where the dead were thought to congregate like meth addicts in public parks. A contemporary Chinese funeral procession whose route takes in a crossroads symbolically bribes its way through.

There was an ulterior motive in putting food and

UNTIL at least the Middle Ages curses were placed in the graves of those whose spirits were thought to have remained and who could be angry enough to be co-opted in bringing bad luck or even death to enemies. The Greeks favored the graves of the young, whose abrupt end almost guaranteed they were still around. The Romans favored the graves of those killed by violence. Racing curses were common—a spirit was thought able to crash chariot teams.

drink in the grave. True enough, the provisions were to sustain the dead on their journey—but they were also to keep the dead occupied so that any harbored resentments, or perhaps plain boredom, didn't turn their minds to mischief. In medieval Europe poppy seeds were craftily included with the grave grub—a narcotic to induce torpor. Several countries, notably Greece and Germany, just as craftily provided knotted strings, in the belief that the dead had an obsession with untying them—and that a single knot took a year to undo. The goods placed in a grave, while meant to be useful either in transit or on arrival, were often broken, so that if it came to it, they couldn't be used against the living. Arctic Europeans and Lapps still drill holes in pots and coins and smash the bottoms of buried boats or break the runners of sleds. Hindus burn the deceased's possessions on the funeral pyre—not as the Chinese do, to forward them to the afterlife address, but to "kill" them and, with them, death contagion.

 ## Welcome Home to the Dead

Throughout recorded history humankind has widely believed that on special days, mostly associated with the intersection of the old and new years, the dead come back to life. And in all cultures feasts for the dead were instituted to show respect—but also to cover the backs of the living, just in case the dead got vindictive. The ancient Romans not only had a feast for the dead but another, the *Lemuria,* specifically for the unhappy dead. It was the original belt-and-suspenders precaution— not that the Romans used either.

The tradition remains powerful in Latin America (the *Día de los Muertos* on the first and second of November); Japan (the Bon Festival, during the seventh month from the night of the thirteenth to the sixteenth); and China (the Festival of Ghosts on the full moon of the seventh lunar month—August by Western calendars).

The Hurons of northeastern America believed that the dead returned collectively once every twelve years, when they held a massive feast.

In the seventh century the pope replaced the old Roman day of the dead with All Saints Day (May 13th);

DURING the three-day *Lemuria,* the feast of those discontented souls that were not at rest, the head of a Roman household got up at midnight and walked barefoot while spitting out nine black beans. If he did not, the *lemure* could carry off any member of his family that it chose.

a hundred years later his successor moved it to November 1st—the Celtic All Hallows Eve or Halloween, when witches and warlocks were thought to be abroad—in a further attempt to stamp out paganism. November 2nd was added as All Souls Day, to honor the ordinary dead. Romania's annual festival of the return of the dead is in February, like ancient Rome's.

In secular Great Britain few people could name the dates of All Saints and All Souls, and the association with Halloween is hazy. But Remembrance Sunday—Poppy Day—commemorating the dead of two world wars still has significance. The British Natural Death Centre now organizes a National Day of the Dead, modeled on Mexico's, on the second Sunday of April each year.

The *Día de los Muertos* as celebrated in Mexico is perhaps the best-known day of the dead (in fact, two days), a mix of Catholic feast days imported by the Spanish conquistadores and Aztec and other native festivals. The living dress up; images of skeletons, skulls, and tombstones parade the streets; and the dead are toasted with lethal *mescal con gusano,* a rougher cousin of tequila that, as its name indicates, has in the bottle the worm that lives at the root of the agave plant from which the drink is made. There's no escaping it: the worm will get you in the end.

 ## Ghosts, Ghouls—and the Undead

Popular opinion has consistently assumed that the overwhelming majority of the dead make the transition from this world to the next smoothly. But some, like vacation travelers at an airport during a strike by air traffic controllers, get stuck. Of these, some wander about helplessly; others get into mischief; and others behave like hooligans.

The West may no longer be prepared to see ghosts everywhere, but otherworldly manifestations remain an aspect of many native cultures, as well as those of China and India. The Chinese believe that unhappy people are reborn as thumb-size spirits called *prets,* who hunger and thirst because what they try to eat turns to fire and ashes; only the ceremony of the burning mouths can release them to be reborn again, in heaven or on earth. Indians believe that while the eternal souls of the dead move on to new bodies in countless rebirths, the lower souls are left behind. These are known as *bhuts,* and until they weaken and are absorbed by the natural elements, they can pose a prob-

IN Ethiopia in 1975 Mengistu Haile Mariam buried his predecessor, the emperor Haile Selassie, under his office floor "to see that the body does not rise from the dead." Zimbabwe's president Robert Mugabe believes he's haunted by the ghost of Josiah Tongogara, who was expected to become president in 1980 but died in a car crash. Mugabe has sought help from witch doctors, a rain goddess, and an oracle, but Tongogara won't go away. Mugabe has an extra place set at dinner each night.

lem. Like *prets* they're essentially harmless, but they can enter the living and cause disease. Because *prets* love milk, no rural mother lets her children out to play after drinking it.

Within Chinese and Hindu thought there's a logic to *prets* and *bhuts,* but there's little explicable in Western thought as to why some of those who've passed over . . . don't. Nothing in the literature suggests that the dead are turned away on the other side. So why is Hamlet's dad not together with the other slain kings, discussing the means of their dispatch the way old ladies discuss their operations? Why is Jacob Marley rattling his chains and not in his Dantean circle with all the other misers? Why some headless horsemen and not other headless horsemen? Why some ladies with lamps, monks, illicit lovers, and not others?

THE second wife of a Hindu must pray for a dead first wife and offer presents. Accordingly the first wife retains her pride, and her *pret* won't persecute her successor. In the Punjab a man about to marry for a second time will initially "marry" a bird, pay a dowry, and then divorce it. If the first wife is vindictive, the bird suffers. If a *bhut* is thought to be the restless soul of one who died unmarried, the solution in south India and Burma is to "marry" it to a living wife.

Who comes back (or stays behind—it depends how you look at it) varies according to the imagination of different cultures, but there are common beliefs. The crossroads corps were always thought to be most likely. So was anyone whose life span had been abruptly terminated by whatever means. And those denied proper burial. Mothers dead in childbirth, mothers taken from young children, children. The irreligious. Those with unfinished business. And of course, the sheer bloody-minded. In India they add the deformed, the insane, and men with-

AFTER his son Christian shot Dag Drollet, his sister's lover, Marlon Brando was reported to say that he was haunted by the dead man's spirit. Sheets flew off Brando's bed, and Drollet's voice came from his car radio saying, "I should not have died."

YOU see what you think you see. . . . The Prussian House of Hohenzollern believed the ghost of a lady in white appeared when the head of the household was about to die. One night in 1708 the third, young—and deranged—wife of family scion King Frederick I broke a glass door and appeared in the bedroom, her nightdress spattered with blood. The old king had a fatal heart attack.

out offspring. In Romania they were convinced that the unreleased sexuality of those who'd died as virgins was almost certain to drive them back for the nookie they'd never had. It might be more accurate to sum up by saying that whether the dead returned as ghosts or ghouls, poltergeists or doppelgängers, shades, apparitions, or bumps in the night—they could be anybody.

In its neurotic way humankind has handled the idea of otherworldly manifestations, but it has been freaked by the possibility of the *revenant*—the corpse reanimated by its original owner or, worse, another. All cultures have been concerned with preventing dead men walking. Commonly potential revenants were buried face down—if they were going to come back to life, they had a lot farther to dig than if buried face up—and had their wrists and legs tied with ropes (a practice echoed in the Chinese tradition of attaching a colored string to the foot of all the dead). Other preventive measures included putting something in the corpse's mouth: wool in ancient Egypt; a potsherd in Prussia; a slip of paper bearing the deceased's name in Poland; a lump of fat among Dakota Indians. Sharp objects— needles, knives, awls, thorned wood—were also tried as in-the-grave deterrents. In Romania, Hungary, and the former Yugoslavia sickles were buried with the body; in Yugoslavia they were placed around the neck, so that if the corpse decided to get up (and presumably turned over), he might decapitate himself. The ancient Greeks didn't fool around: they chopped off the extremities of murderers and victims—the most likely walkers, in their opinion—and hung them around their necks.

Until medieval times Jews and Christians stopped an active revenant by cremation. After that, while Serbs cut the corpse's knee ligaments and Icelanders drove nails into the soles of the feet, the universal method

ARCHAEOLOGISTS believe that early coffins were secured with far more nails (expensive items) than were strictly necessary to keep the lid on.

THE revenant as vampire is not, as popularly supposed, part of the folk belief of only Transylvania (now in Romania but in Hungary until 1918). Vampires are known in India (the *baital* is half man, half bat), in Africa (the *asanbosom* has hooks for feet and bites its victims on the thumb), and in Crete (the *kathakano* can only be killed by boiling the decapitated head in vinegar).

The Transylvanian tradition became known in the West only in 1746 when a French monk wrote a credulous treatise. Sheridan Le Fanu *(In a Glass Darkly,* 1872) and Bram Stoker *(Dracula,* 1897) turned it into best sellers, which became the stuff of countless films from the silent *Nosferatu* and the Hammer horrors to *Interview with a Vampire.*

In Haitian folklore zombies are the dead reanimated (though *animated* is definitely not the word) by voodoo. It's less a case of resurrection, it's suggested, than drug-induced brain damage.

was the stake hammered into the grave or even the corpse. Later still the Greeks uniquely favored firing a shot into the coffin. Plunging a stake through the heart was the preventive action used against suicides in Britain where, evidently, they were considered as dangerous as the ancient Greeks considered murderers and murder victims. Law forbade the practice only in 1823.

Attractions of Death

In the Middle Ages monks carved their own coffins, and until relatively recent times some orders slept in theirs as a constant reminder of the transience of life. Victorian poets who devoted much of their output to death tried sleeping in coffins to sharpen their creative insight. Today young Goths in Dracula black and graveyard makeup have taken to coffin napping to complete their post–punk commitment to morbidity. In all three cases the activity is hardly mainstream, but it does show that pre-mortem associations have attractions for some.

Indeed, someone else's potential demise can be an aphrodisiac. It was to millions of women in the last century's two world wars, who didn't hold back from giving what they had to give to men going off to fight and who might not return. It has been for the dozens of women attracted into correspondence and then marriage with residents of death row. What goes around comes around: two thousand years ago Roman matrons were

 YOU can buy a corpse from Distephano Enterprises in Wilmington, Delaware, modeled in realistic detail, in latex. Choice of sex, skin, and hair color—and degree of decomposition. Cost: $650.

nipping down to the Colosseum for a gladiatorial quickie. It's rather cheering to think that "they who were about to die" raised a salute before the one they gave the emperor.

For millennia death dominated humankind's thoughts. Now, by and large, we leave death to work its side of the street, and we work ours. A wise man, the philosopher Spinoza said, doesn't think about death. Actually, the West has gone beyond Spinoza. The Victorians constructed an elaborate system of social ritual to deal with death—backed with an array of mourning clothes and artifacts, including black-edged stationery and handkerchiefs, fans and jewelry, even antimacassars and teapots—that remained in place well into the twentieth century. Today that's been reduced to not much more than a "sorry for your sad loss" card. To us, the Victorian period of prolonged mourning is faintly bizarre—our bereaved are more likely to go on vacation. As recently as the 1930s rural British communities rang a "passing bell" from the parish church when someone lay on their deathbed— six times for a woman, nine for a man, followed by a peal for each year of the dying person's life; the death knell was rung at the moment of internment. Now "we hurry the dead without observance, disposing of them like the household rubbish." That, you might feel, is

LIKE the ancient Egyptians, the Eskimos of Hudson Bay and the Patani Malay people believe that during sleep the soul leaves the body, which is why they think it dangerous to awaken a person, whose soul may thereby be "lost."

going a bit far, but it's undeniable that, broadly speaking, we have become a death-denying society. Only Mexico, perhaps, with its vivid clash of cultures, long history of bloodshed, and poverty, is still, as the poet Octavio Paz writes, "seduced by death."

Earlier civilizations regarded sleep as the brother of death, and it remains its metaphor. "Awake," Macduff shouts to Malcolm and Banquo in *Macbeth,* after the murder of King Duncan. "Shake off this downy sleep, death's counterfeit / And look at death itself." Look? Not if we can help it—we've excluded death from polite society and find it naïve that it was once believed that gods and the elite dead dropped into the dreams of kings, priests, and heroes. And yet we can't prevent death from occasionally gate-crashing our unguarded minds. Modern psychology's position on the subject is that a dream involving someone else's death might just be a premonition; if it involves your own, it's much more likely to be about something in your life that requires fundamental change than a shot across your bow from the Grim Terminator. There are exceptions, as there always are. The night before he died, Abraham Lincoln dreamed he entered the East Wing of the White House and saw himself in his coffin. When he asked what had happened, he was told that he'd been assassinated. Unfortunately the dream didn't tell him not to go to the theater.

Would Lincoln have believed that, had he been told it by someone else? Would you believe something similar involving yourself? Or would you put a bad dream down to the erratic communication of unattended thought processes combined, perhaps, with a dodgy late-night take-out?

 ## Is There Anyone There?

The ancients seem to have had little trouble contacting the dead even when they weren't sleeping. If they didn't visit the dead in the underworld, the dead came to them, often conjured up to foretell the future as Samuel

 IN Brazil, where Spiritism is a religion, *The Spirits Book*, published in 1857 by a Frenchman, sells as many copies as the Bible.

was at the behest of Saul, the first king of Israel—who wished he hadn't bothered, because the message was that he was to lose his job to David, have his ass kicked by the Philistine army, and by the following evening be back at Samuel's place with his sons.

Necromancy, or prophesying by calling up the dead, was widely practiced in all cultures, was occasionally banned when incidents heightened trepidation, and was finally condemned by the Church in medieval Europe when it was associated with black magic. Some went to the stake for continuing with it, but it remained common into the Renaissance and beyond. In the nineteenth century spiritualism had the novel idea of gathering up the souls of the dead and putting them on a plane that enjoyed a higher level of existence but that was not to be confused with heaven or hell. This notion revived interest in communicating with those on the other side of the curtain. Begun in 1848 in America, but quickly embraced by England, spiritualism filled darkened Victorian drawing rooms with groups of people who frightened themselves with automatic writing, table turning, and rapping (no, not that—knocking on wood). The craze remained in vogue for about forty years (with at its peak in the U.S. more than two million American enthusiasts), while in Europe a surge of interest in contacting the dead followed at the end of the

Great War, fell back, then revived for the same reasons during and after the Second World War (there were a million British adherents of spiritualism in 1944, with a thousand churches and an estimated fifty thousand home circles), and then declined once more. Now re-labeled *idionecrophany,* it attracts some interest, but so do crop circles, UFOs, and alien pregnancies.

An analysis of social surveys in the United States that asked if people had had contact with "variable spirits" found that 22 percent thought that they had

AT a séance held by a "materialization" medium, ectoplasm emanated from his or her (usually her) nose, mouth, or clothes and took on semisolid form, with features that willing onlookers could recognize. From time to time sitters attempted to snip or wrench away pieces of this milky emission for laboratory analysis. Tests were often inconclusive: it was fine muslin, paper fibers bound with egg white—or a substance unknown. The Society for Psychical Research was founded in 1882 by a selection of eminent Victorians who attempted to establish an investigative framework for what might be a new branch of science. Former Prime Minister William Gladstone and novelist Arthur Conan Doyle were members. Conan Doyle also believed in reincarnation and predicted he'd reappear at the Albert Hall several weeks after his death; the 10,000 people who turned up were disappointed.

once or twice, 10 percent more frequently, and 4 percent often. There were more women than men, and more Catholics than Protestants. Americans are roughly twice as likely as Germans, Italians, Poles, and Brits to think they've been in touch with someone on the other side—and four times more likely than Norwegians and Russians, who definitely seem to think idionecrophany is missing a *t*. No one would deny it's a good Scrabble word, though.

Worldwide, more than thirty thousand people belong to societies dedicated to taping voices from beyond using cassette recorders—variable speed at the top of the range, because the dead apparently sometimes speak very fast and sometimes have to be played backward. But channeling—the séance with a makeover—remains the most frequent means of attempting to establish contact and still requires the services of a medium, someone who claims the gift of affinity with the dead and the ability, in a trancelike state, to reach out to them. Mediumship is the message. And the "is there anybody there?" business hasn't stood still. There's electronic monitoring now, e-mails to heaven (unsuccessful ones returned "host not found"), and communication by computer spellcheck. Don't you just love I.T.?

If you're not a believer, it's as well to remember

Kant's observation that he doubted every story of otherworldly manifestation individually, but somehow believed in the whole of them together. Samuel Johnson noted that "all argument is against it but all belief is for it." What's disappointing is that even when a connection is apparently made to the greatest minds (Kant's and Johnson's perhaps) they seem to have little to say about anything, including where they are—a bit like teenagers calling each other on their cell phones. And invariably they sound like a distorted Speak 'n' Spell.

 ## Rest in Pieces

Once the touch of a still-warm corpse was thought to cure sickness—another reason, other than the entertainment value, why executions were well attended. When a corpse was cut down, there was a rush to reach it. In the mid-seventeenth century a Frenchman in London noted "a young woman, with an appearance of beauty, all pale and trembling, in the arms of the executioner, who submitted to have her bosom uncovered in the presence of thousands of spectators and the dead man's hand placed upon it." In medieval and Renaissance Europe the corpse of anyone who'd met a premature or violent death was thought to retain a measure of unused vitality, and their body parts be-

MOVING to San Jose, California, after the death of her rifle manufacturer husband in 1918, Sarah Winchester contacted him through a medium and was told that as long as she kept building her home, she would never face death. By the time she had to—at 85—the original 17-room mansion had 150 rooms, 13 bathrooms, 2,000 doors, 47 fireplaces, and 10,000 windows.

came ingredients in charms and medicines; three hundred years ago a severed hand could command a price of ten guineas.

Historically, all religions believed in the physical and spiritual power of the bodies of holy people and, while the whole was more than the parts, happily chopped them up to broadcast their efficacy as widely as possible. Buddha ordered his body cut into eight pieces and enshrined in stupas where they'd do the most good— at crossroads. A temple dedicated to one of the Buddha's teeth is in Sri Lanka; Istanbul houses a finger of the Prophet. Christianity was no less enthusiastic: from the fifth century, when the catacombs fell out of use, remains were removed and placed as relics in churches, and down the centuries tombs of martyrs were raided. Heads, hearts, and entrails were frequently buried in different places—very useful in the

THE great and the good were likely to go to the grave without some anatomical component—or lose something while there. Einstein went without his brain, which he'd donated to science. Napoleon went without his penis, which was illegally removed at his autopsy, as were four vertebrae from Charles I at his belated autopsy in 1813—novelist Sir Walter Scott had them made into a saltshaker. Henry VIII had already gone to his tomb without a finger; it was stolen by a workman when the body was being interred in the royal vault at Windsor Castle, and made into a knife handle. In the eighteenth century a gravedigger named Elizabeth Grant was charging visitors to view John Milton's teeth and a part of his leg.

Among those who went headless to the grave: Austrian composer Joseph Haydn (two friends bribed the gravedigger to let them keep his—but he and it were reunited 145 years later); Sir Walter Raleigh (his widow kept his for 30 years after his execution, and it went to the grave later with his son Carew); and King Charles XII of Sweden (the skull is on public display in Stockholm, complete with bullet hole made in 1718). The artist Goya had his head when first buried, but when he was exhumed from a cemetery in Bordeaux and transferred to his native Spain, it went missing somewhere along the way and hasn't been seen since.

Among those who went heartless: the poet Shelley, whose heart was retrieved from his cremation pyre on an Italian beach by his friend Trelawney and was kept by Shelley's wife Mary, dried and pressed flat in a book of his poetry; and the writer Thomas Hardy.

> He had wanted a simple burial in his home village, but the nation wanted him in Westminster Abbey. The compromise was that his heart went back to Dorset—but his sister left it on the kitchen table, and her cat ate it.

case of Saint Ethelbert, whose head was elsewhere in 1050 when the Danes razed Hereford. Bishop Aymer de Valence had his heart deposited separately from the rest of him in Winchester Cathedral. Saint Catherine of Siena was decapitated after her death in 1380 so that her head could remain in the city when her body was interred in Rome. In 1461 the head of Saint Andrew was given as a gift to Pope Pius II. Old habits: part of the intestines of Pope John Paul II, removed during surgery after a failed assassination attempt in 1981, were interred in the Church of Santi Vincenzo e Anastasio.

Medieval Europe was reliquary mad. Ordinary citizens wore amulets or medallions containing ashes, bones, hair, or skin. Armies rode into battle waving body parts— Robert the Bruce attributed his famous victory at Bannockburn in 1314 to the arm of Saint Fillan. Churches attempted to steal one another's relics and were sometimes taken for a ride. The brain of Saint Peter, which for centuries was housed above an altar in Geneva, turned out to be pumice stone. Even today thirteen churches in different countries claim to have Jesus's foreskin, which suggests at least twelve fakes or an unrecorded miracle on a par with the loaves and fishes.

 ## Grave Robbing: The Oldest Profession?

Grave robbery might well be an older profession than harlotry and has caused humanity great anxiety. People worried that the plundering of graves might prevent the dead's onward journey—and might incur their wrath, causing their spirits to rise up. It's hardly surprising that since earliest times attempts have been made to make tombs and coffins robbery-proof.

Egyptian architects produced complex labyrinths leading to burial chambers constructed like bomb shelters. The builders filled work shafts with rubble, blocked entrances with sliding slabs and portcullises, and cunningly deployed blind passages, booby traps, and ingenious locking systems. The Egyptians also plastered their tombs with curses inside and out—which had as much effect as "Do not walk on the grass" notices. As for the defenses, the tomb raiders simply tunneled through the masonry at random until they found a way in, then made off with everything they could carry. In the early centuries A.D. even the outer casings of smooth white limestone that covered the

IN 1922 when Howard Carter excavated Tutankhamen's tomb, there was wide public conjecture as to whether curses could work.

Supposedly, when Carter's team broke through, a cobra swallowed his canary, the start of a seven-year period during which eleven members of the team, including Carter, died. Curse? Mosquito bites? A German microbiologist believes that the food provided in Egyptian tombs grew poisonous mold spores, which rose into the air when the tomb was opened.

pyramids were stolen—the Great Pyramid is now three hundred feet short of its original height.

Records suggest that much of the thieving during Egypt's long history was conducted or masterminded by those on the inside—the masons who knew the layout of the tombs, and the undertakers. Radiography reveals that many mummies were robbed in the embalming workshop: only the impressions of their bodily jewelry and amulets were left in the bandages, which had been unwound and then rewound. As the various amulets (seven commonly, one hundred forty-three in King Tut's case) had covered the corpse's organs and limbs for specific reasons—providing heat, assisting later suppleness, underwriting everlasting life—their loss seriously compromised the dead's future chances; and the loss of the most valuable amulet of all, the scarab or dung beetle associated with the heart, the site of an individual's identity, was catastrophic.

History repeats itself. In Europe during much of the second millennium more insiders were on the make. Church sextons often had a nice little earner going, in league with the gravediggers, pocketing any valuables they found on the dead. These were easy pickings in the centuries of shrouds and shallow burials. Grave robbery was so rife that when coffins came into fashion, the rich and the better-off tried having them made tamper-proof, with hingeless lids, unopenable fastenings, even made wholly of metal—but with conspicuous lack of success. There's little in this world that can stand in the way of determination and a hefty hammer. One interesting idea to thwart thieves in the late eighteenth century was a cemetery gun, rigged to fire when someone tripped it, but it wasn't exactly discriminating and had to be banned by law.

Grave robbing has never gone away. In Java in 1998 gangs of grave robbers armed with saws and crowbars dug up 268 Chinese graves in two cities, taking not only valuables but many of the coffins, too; in Colombia it's reported that a grave robber can earn up to $15,000 a year, a huge sum matched only by exporting drugs.

And on a loftier plane, the museums of the world continue to condone the practice—except in that case it's called archaeology.

Body Snatching: A Nice Little Earner

The theft of corpses has brought even more disquiet than tomb raiding. Egyptian mummies were sometimes taken from their resting place, to be unwrapped at leisure for their spoils, and without its body base the soul of its owner was thought lost. Medieval humankind struggled in the grip of a superstition that wasn't dissimilar and also worried that their loved ones might be dug up for use in the black arts. But no age was ever as gripped by worry about body snatching as the Victorians.

The Renaissance had begun to change attitudes toward dissection of the human body, but even in the nineteenth century the only legal source of corpses was

IN 280 B.C. two Greek physicians named Erasistratus and Herophilus dissected the bodies of prisoners of war—while they were still conscious. The unfortunates were flayed and cut apart so that their organs could be seen in situ.

the gallows—which in an era of intellectual curiosity and advances in all fields including medicine wasn't enough to keep up with demand.

"Resurrection men" or body snatchers had been supplying the medical schools of Europe with their raw materials in the eighteenth century, but now it became a wholesale activity. A loophole in the law allowed the trade: taking only a corpse was a misdemeanor, whereas taking a corpse's clothes or possessions was a felony. Body snatching was lucrative—so much so that undertakers were known to work with resurrectionists. One private burial ground in London was owned by an anatomist who had a double income from those paying for what they thought was a secure burial and from his students who paid for fresh specimens.

Self-employed resurrectionists could earn a good living from the dead: £4 a pop, a month's wages for a laborer. In Edinburgh Dr. Robert Knox at the university medical school—where as many as five hundred students attended his classes—paid as much as £10, a sum so irresistible it launched the careers of Burke and Hare. Ulstermen who'd come to Scotland as laborers on the Union Canal, the Williams Burke and Hare began body snatching from the usual sources, then hit on the idea that they could save themselves the digging, and command the best prices, by converting the living into

A LONG line of the famous have been snatched from their graves—for postmortem retribution. They include Thomas à Becket, who died in 1170, was exhumed in 1540, and was then burned as punishment for high treason against Henry II; Voltaire was stolen from his sarcophagus opposite Rousseau's in the Pantheon for his religious cynicism and thrown in the city dump (but his heart is in the national library in Paris); and Thomas Paine was refused a Quaker cemetery and was then taken from the resting place he did get, for his revolutionary zeal.

Strangest of all, Oliver Cromwell, lord high protector of England, was yanked out of his spot in Westminster Abbey after the restoration of the monarchy, hanged as a traitor, beheaded, and had his head used as a football before being displayed on a spike for two years. Passing through many hands in the next three hundred years, his head was finally buried at his old college, Sidney Sussex, Cambridge.

cadavers—which they proceeded to do, utilizing a barrel of water so as to leave as little trace of violence as possible. The murder of their sixteenth victim led to their arrest. Hare turned king's evidence, and Burke went to the gallows—and thence back to the medical school one last time. His skeleton is still on display there.

Lynch mobs and watchtowers in some graveyards

didn't stop the flow of bodies, but the Anatomy Act of 1832, three years after the Burke and Hare scandal, did. The poor, however, weren't happy—those who died in hospitals and workhouses were to be the new source of surgical specimens.

Body snatching has continued for reasons that earlier centuries would find familiar. In 1975 the *New York Times* exposed a ring that was taking corpses from cemeteries in order to be able to collect a portion of the state burial allowance for the homeless. In 1992 Colombian police broke up a Burke-and-Hare-style gang supplying the Free University of Barranquilla with indigents; the university's medical institute was closed down. In 2000 the remains of Hannes Rall, a deputy minister of transport in the South African apartheid regime, was dug up because of the belief that the crushed bones of well-known

 THERE are fewer organ donors than are needed—and more people than can be used want to leave the whole of themselves to medical science, for use in orthopedic research and new emergency techniques, for instance, and to give the next generation of doctors hands-on experience. The Uniform Anatomical Gift Act adopted by most states only permits the use of bodies that have been bequeathed in wills or verbally agreed with the relatives before a death. Medical schools aren't allowed to purchase a body.

whites could be made into a tea cure for AIDS. The following year remains were removed from graves in South Vietnam, on a rumor that the U.S. government was paying a reward for missing GIs.

In a story that made world headlines in 1977, Charlie Chaplin, who'd died at eighty-eight a couple of months earlier, was snatched from the Swiss village cemetery at Corsier-sur-Vevy by two eastern European political refugees who wanted a $600,000 ransom so that they could open a garage. Chaplin's widow refused, even when the demand dropped to $250,000; when the pair were caught, coffin and occupant came back from a cornfield ten miles away. There have been other raids on the graves of the famous, including Abraham Lincoln's in 1876—a gang hoping to get a forger friend out of prison were apprehended in the act. Which is why Abe is now well concreted in. In 1987, thirteen years after his death, General Juan Perón was dug up and had his hands removed for an $8-million ransom—which was not forthcoming from the Argentine government. In 1991 that portion of Buddha deposited in Nepal was filched for sale on the international black market. In a curious case in 1992 the body of Ransom Olds (of Oldsmobile fame) was taken from the tomb in which it had lain for almost forty years. Nothing more was heard—no Ransom, so to speak.

Buried Alive

If the Victorians were unhappy about grave robbing and horrified by body snatching, they were hysterical about being buried alive. So were their contemporaries in Germany, France, and America.

Since classical antiquity some observers were aware that the criteria of death could be fallible. In the eighteenth century, when medical opinion was slowly coming to the realization that cases of sudden death could sometimes be reversed, and resuscitation techniques were beginning to be employed—humane societies sprang up, to give artificial respiration to swimmers feared drowned—people were more ready than ever to believe that the living just might end up six feet under.

TRUE OR FALSE? In the sixth century on Iona (a Scottish island), one of St. Columba's monks, Oran, was found to be alive after having been buried. When he told his fellow monks he had seen heaven and hell, he was promptly dispatched and reinterred on grounds of heresy. In the thirteenth century Thomas à Kempis, reputed author of *The Imitation of Christ,* did not achieve sainthood because when they dug up his body for the ossuary, they found scratch marks on the lid of the coffin and concluded that he was not reconciled to his fate.

Well-meaning alarmists gave advice. As a result, on expiration the dead had the juices of onions, garlic, and horseradish shoved up their noses, nettles applied to their skin, vinegar and salt poured into their mouths, and their ears shocked "by hideous Shrieks and excessive Noises." They even had the soles of their feet cut with razors and needles thrust under their toenails.

In the nineteenth century fear of premature burial reached fever pitch, and there were tales aplenty to make people's hair stand on end. Scratch marks on the lids of disinterred coffins. Exhumed corpses that had eaten off their fingers. Corpses in violent contortions of failed escape. Coffins broken open from the inside. Buried corpses heard to cry out.

The only certain indication of death was putrefaction. Some followed the example of the bishop of

HANNA Beswick of Lancashire, England, was so frightened of being buried alive that she ensured she wasn't buried at all. When she went at the age of 77 in 1758, she was embalmed and placed inside a grandfather clock, with a velvet curtain over the glass viewing panel where her face was. Just over a hundred years later the trustees of her estate agreed she wasn't now likely to show signs of life, and had her interred.

Cloyne, who in the previous century had left instructions that his body be kept aboveground for a full five days. The earl of Lytton directed that he wasn't to be coffined or even moved from his bed until three medical men had declared in writing that the signs of decomposition were unmistakable. In Germany Kaiser Wilhelm I ordered the provision of "waiting mortuaries" at cemeteries, where the dead could lie on stretchers "supervised for at least seventy-two hours." The waiting mortuaries were not a great success. The poor feared their relatives would be snatched from them for medical experimentation, while the rich spurned them because they thought it undignified to allow their dead to lie naked in low company.

Another stratagem was the fitting of coffins with alarm systems. The most common had strings attached to the hands of corpses, which were then attached to bells (as they were in the waiting mortuary), so that the dead—if they weren't—could call for room service. The most comprehensive had a spring-loaded ball on the corpse's chest so that any movement would release a trap door in the lid to admit air and light, raise a flag, ring a bell (that would sound for thirty minutes), and light a lamp to burn after sunset. The most ingenious and probably most wildly impractical (U.S. patent number 81,437, issued August 25, 1868, to inventor Franz Vester of

IN the late sixteenth century, when the body of Matthew Wall was being borne to his grave in Braughing, England, a pallbearer tripped—and Wall revived in the dropped coffin. He lived for several more years, celebrating his "resurrection" each year until his final departure in 1595. Margorie Halcrow Erskin of Chirnside, Scotland, was buried in 1674. When the sexton was trying to cut off her finger to remove a ring, she sat up. In her additional years she gave birth to two sons, Ralph and Ebenezer Erskine, founders of the Secession Church of Berwickshire. In 1724 in Musselburgh, Scotland, relatives determined to bury Maggie Dickson, who'd just been hanged, got into a fight with a party of medical students who wanted her body. During the mélee Dickson revived—and lived another thirty years, nicknamed "Half Hangit."

Newark, New Jersey) involved a sliding door and a shaft housing a ladder. A patent for an alarmed coffin was taken out as recently as 1983.

For 150 years or so *taphophobia*—fear of premature burial—was endemic, even among the educated. George Washington was a taphophobe, as was novelist Wilkie Collins, who carried a letter imploring anyone finding him dead to contact a doctor for a second opinion. Another was the opera composer Giacomo Meyerbeer, who was, in fact, buried in a string-and-bell coffin. Others took preburial measures. Many saw to it that a gun, knife, or poison went into the ground with them, and writers Edmund Yates and Harriet Martineau left money to their doctors, in the one instance to slit his jugular, in the other to cut off her head.

Today the scratch marks once found inside coffin lids are mostly ascribed to postdeath contractions, missing body parts to rodents, and contorted corpses and burst coffins to the pressure of decomposition gases, which also explains the claim that corpses have been heard to scream. Yet in the sixteenth and seventeenth centuries epidemics of plague, cholera, and smallpox are known to have caused comas that on occasion were taken for death, and fear of contagion meant that burials were often carried out with great haste. Exaggerated or not, a seventeenth-century source compiled 219 cases of narrow escape from pre-

URBAN MYTH: The phrase "saved by the bell" doesn't derive from coffins with sounding devices. It's a boxing term from the 1930s.

URBAN MYTH: Hair and nails don't grow in the coffin—the illusion is created by the retraction of the skin.

mature burial, 149 of premature burial, and ten of bodies being dissected and found to be still breathing. The epidemics of the Victorian era—coupled with the squalid nature of the funeral business and the possibilities of misdiagnosis of death in cases of coma induced by accidents involving new mechanical machines or newfangled electricity—make it likely that others suffered the same fate. We shouldn't be surprised. Doctors can still be as spectacularly incompetent in pronouncing death as their counterparts in earlier centuries, as the cases of the apparently dead sitting up on mortuary slabs or even on dissecting tables testify.

In the early days of commercial embalming, sales-

DECLARED dead after a traffic accident in Johannesburg, South Africa, in 1993, Sipho Mdletshe spent two days in a metal box in a mortuary before his cries alerted workers. His fiancée wouldn't have anything to do with him, saying he was a zombie who'd returned from the dead to haunt her. In 1994 86-year-old Mildred Clarke, pronounced dead after being found on her living-room floor, spent 90 minutes in a body bag in the morgue at the Albany Medical Center Hospital before an attendant detected that the coroner was in error—the bag was breathing. In 2001 a man who was buried in Kazakhstan after being electrocuted while stealing power cables turned up at his own wake.

men used to recommend the procedure to potential customers on the grounds that it guaranteed you were really dead before you got in your coffin. That's one sales pitch that remains true. But cremation is ecologically sounder and just as good a guarantee that you won't hear the wriggling approach of what Poe called "Conqueror Worm."

NDEs: Back to the Future?

In 1975 America discovered that maybe you could die and then return: that you could be clinically dead—no heartbeat, no brain activity—and then turn back from death's door. The enthusiasm for the near-death experience was stimulated by Raymond Moody's book *Life After Life,* which chronicled the case histories of 150 people who believed they'd done just that. The idea that it might be possible to experience death on a try-before-you-buy basis was attractive to many people and remains so. In fact, the idea is as old as humanity. Leaving Lazarus out of it, there are accounts galore from Plato to Bede, Tolstoy to Jung—even Hemingway; Eastern thought has been no less drawn to the belief that some are given a glimpse of the afterlife.

Near-death experiences (NDEs) vary, but the common pattern is that the dead/dying (there's a problem of past and continuous present here) feel the self leave the body and float above it, move through a dark tunnel toward a bright light, meet deceased relatives or others, have visions of past and future life, and despite a profound sense of peace with what seems to be, finally turn back at a barrier. Science interprets all this less euphorically. The tunnel and bright light result from the back of the eye being starved of oxygen, causing the nerve cells to fire at random; the floating, the encounters, and the visions are the sputter of the brain's electric impulses, little different from dreaming; and the turning back isn't an indication of a heavenly reprieve but a tribute to modern resuscitation skills.

Those who believe they've had an NDE are not shaken by these explanations, or by the question why, during their out-of-body floating in the operating theater—when they watch and listen to the medical staff struggling to save them—they haven't noticed items on tops of cupboards put there by sneaky investigators. On the other hand science can't answer why, if NDEs are nothing more than the physiological shutdown of the body's functions, not everyone diagnosed as being clinically kaput has them. According to the latest research, only one in five do. And whatever science says, those experiencing an NDE return to life with a strong sense of having to do something more with it, and an equanimity about facing up to the real thing when it arrives. Having been there and done that, they know what to expect—a bit like work experience, really.

NOT SO GRIM REMINDERS

At birth we cry; at death we see why.
—Bulgarian proverb

 Quipping Death into Shape

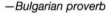

Death has inspired more human creativity than anything except love. Before his own suicide Arthur
Koestler wrote:

> *If the word death was absent from our vocabu-*
> *lary, our great works of literature would have re-*
> *mained unwritten, pyramids and cathedrals*
> *would not exist, nor works of religious art—and*
> *all art is of religious or magic origin. The pathol-*
> *ogy and creativity of the human mind are two*

sides of the same medal, coined by the same mintmaster.

There's no escaping death, in more ways than the obvious one. Death is in the news, in novels, in music, in films. Death is in your face. And wouldn't it be depressing if we didn't joke about it? The living are the dead on vacation, we say. Death is life's way of telling us to slow down, we say. Who in the Western world hasn't heard Woody Allen's most famous quip: "I'm not afraid to die. I just don't want to be there when it happens"? We do relish the death-defying quip. Even those who have the

GENEVA, SWITZERLAND—Despite the enormous efforts of doctors, rescue workers, and other medical professionals worldwide, the global death rate remains constant at 100%.

Death, a metabolic affliction causing total shutdown of all life functions, has long been considered humanity's number-one health concern. The condition has no cure.

"I was really hoping, what with all those new radiology treatments, rescue helicopters, aerobics TV shows, and what have you, that we might at least make a dent in it this year," World Health Organization director general Dr. Gernst Bladt said.

—www.gagpipe.com, "Headline Satire from Around the World"

Grim Reaper standing in the room tapping his watch can be humorous about their fate, if they have the wit. When the great Puritan John Owen was on his deathbed, dictating a letter, his secretary wrote for him: "I am still in the land of the living." "Stop," Owen said as this was read back. "Change it to say, I am yet in the land of the dying, but I hope soon to be in the land of the living." Following a stroke, the former U.S. president John Quincy Adams told a fellow congressman who inquired about his health: "I inhabit a weak, frail, decayed tenement, battered by the winds and broken in upon by the storm, and for all I can learn, the landlord does not intend to repair." The English novelist Somerset Maugham, irritated that he was taking so long to die, told his nephew that dying was a dreary affair, adding: "My advice to you is to have nothing whatsoever to do with it."

That death comes to everyone has been a subject of grim humor since ancient times. The satirist Lucian poked fun at the skull of Helen of Troy, observing that even beauty was given no dispensation. In the mid-fourteenth century in Europe, when the plague killed so many people that the population didn't return to the same level for nearly two hundred years, death was seen as macabre comedy—it was that or go mad, a contemporary diarist noted.

TEN paintings about death: *At the Last Judgment,* Rogier van der Weyden (1400–64); *The Death of the Miser,* Hieronymus Bosch (1450–1516); *The Triumph of Death,* Pieter Brueghel the Elder (1530–69); *The Beheading of John the Baptist,* Caravaggio (1573–1610); *The Death of Marat,* Jacques-Louis David (1748–1825); *The Third of May,* Francisco de Goya (1746–1828); *The Vale of Rest,* John Millais (1829–96); *The Suicide,* Edouard Manet (1832–83); *The Child,* Max Klinger (1857–1920); *The Best Doctor,* Alfred Kubin (1877–1959).

Oddly, a pantomime performed in French churches saved the collective sanity. The *danse Mácabre,* in which skeletons dragged the living down into the grave, was staged because in the ecclesiastical view it focused the mind on religious duty. But the idea had such satirical possibilities that by the Renaissance dancing skeletons were everywhere, like modern cartoons. The forty-one woodcuts made by Hans Holbein the Younger were the period's ultimate comment on death, showing stereotypical figures from emperor to child, from clerk to miser, each representing a vice, taking part in a deathly dust-up with their bony Pied Pipers. The woodcuts were suppressed for nearly twenty years—nine of the figures portrayed belonged to the Church.

The king and the pawn go back into the same box

when the game is over, runs an Italian saying from the time. So do popes, cardinals, and parish priests. And so do artists who wield a wicked chisel—Holbein died of the plague.

 ## Words, Words, Words

We never notice how death and the afterlife stitch our conversations together. We'll "catch our death," we're "in seventh heaven," we "go to hell and back." We "never say die." *Dead* as an adjective is not only as dead as a dodo or a doornail, it's a favorite, qualifying countless words—including, recently and not entirely logically, *good*. But language often isn't logical: why do we say "a hell of a nice fellow"—isn't that contradictory?

Considering that the Greeks and Romans have given us most of the vocabulary, as well as the customs, of death, it's intriguing that *death* itself is Old Norse in origin. *Cemetery* in Greek and Latin is "sleeping place." *Coffin* comes from the Greek for "basket"— the early Greeks, like the Sumerians, buried their dead in baskets woven from plaited twigs. *Epitaph,* from the Greek, means "on the tomb." *Funeral* (from torch), *mortuary* (dead), *cremation* (burn), and *ossuary* (bones) all derive from Latin. So does *columbarium,* which has

OF the 10 most popular operas (9 really—the one-acters *Cavalleria Rusticana* and *I Pagliacci* come as a pair), 7 feature at least one death: *Carmen* (stabbed heroine); *Aïda* (hero buried alive, heroine hides to join him); *La Traviata* (heroine claimed by consumption); *La Bohème* (ditto); *Tosca* (stabbed villain, shot hero, heroine a suicide jumper); *I Pagliacci* (stabbed heroine); *Rigoletto* (heroine substitutes herself for her seducer in dad's revenge).

Outside the top 10 (9), few operas are complete without death (including, of course, anything adapted from Shakespeare), with heroines committing suicide in, for example, *L'Africaine, Lakmé, La Gioconda Gotterdämmerung, Il Trovatore, Turandot,* and *La Wally.* In *Lucia di Lammermoor* the hero stabs himself on the heroine's tomb; in *Ernani* the hero stabs himself in fulfillment of a pledge to die when his enemy sounds his horn (don't ask).

No one has investigated whether opera has inspired suicide, but Goethe's original story of Werther—in which the lovelorn hero shoots himself—prompted a wave of last exits across Europe.

And the 3 in the top 10 not involving death: Rossini's *The Barber of Seville;* Mozart's *The Marriage of Figaro*—and *Cavalleria Rusticana.*

many niches for holding urns of ashes and looks like a dovecote—the original meaning. *Sarcophagus* from the Greek is "flesh eater"—a figurative reference to the rapidity with which bodies interred in porous limestone repositories decay to bones. *Cenotaph* is also from the Greek—literally "empty grave," a monument to those whose bodies are unrecovered.

Etymologically *hearse* has come into the language via a circuitous route from Latin through Anglo-French. Introduced into western Europe by the Romans, the *hirpex*, or "rake," was called a *harrow* in the British Isles. Under the Normans the pronunciation became *herse*, and ecclesiastical candelabra that resembled the inverted implement began to be referred to by the word. In the fifteenth century *herse* candelabra were mounted on the lid of a coffin in the funeral cortege; and in the following century, when the word, now *hearse*, was transferred to the wheeled cart on which the coffin was carried, the rake's progress was complete.

 IN the last 500 years a number of choral masterpieces have been written as requiem masses for the dead. Among those who've turned their hand to the requiem (Latin for "rest") are Mozart, Berlioz, Cherubini, Verdi, Dvořák, Bruckner, and Fauré. In the twentieth century Delius derived his libretto from the German philosopher Nietzsche. The *War Requiem* of the British composer Benjamin Britten contains poetry by Wilfred Owen, killed in the First World War, linking the work to the senseless suffering of war.

IDIOMATIC death: To have one foot in the grave is to be at death's door—the ancient Greek phrase was "with one foot in the ferryboat." To pass through the door is to give up the ghost/turn one's face to the wall/fall off the perch/head for the last roundup/go the way of all flesh/to meet one's maker/to glory or kingdom come or the happy hunting ground/or join the choir invisible. These are self-explanatory phrases, as are probably *croak* (the death rattle), *snuff it* (like a candle) or *bite the dust* (though this was an expression for dying in a fall from a horse centuries before we associated it with cowboys and Indians). But how many people know that the origin of *curtains* was the custom of drawing curtains around a bed when someone in it had just died; that *peg out* comes from the game of cribbage; and that *pop your clogs* once meant pawning your footwear? There are varying explanations for *kick the bucket:* one suggestion is that it comes from Old French for "beam" or "yoke"; more colorfully, that a bucket was what many suicides who hanged themselves stood on and then kicked away; and a third that in East Anglia a *bucket* was the frame from which a newly killed pig was suspended.

Poetic turns of phrase for death: "kind Nature's signal to retreat" (Johnson); "the journey's end" and "a knell that summons thee to heaven or to hell" (Shakespeare); "that dreamless sleep" (Byron); "the pale priest of the mute people" (Browning). Tennyson described death as "put to sea," but the navy has many similar allusions, including "slip one's wind" and "coil up your cable." A rather nice military one is "to lose the number of one's mess."

SOME argot associated with death has a long history: the hearse as a *meat wagon,* the coffin as a *bone box* or *six-foot bungalow* (surprisingly, seventeenth century), the cemetery as a *bone yard* or *marble city,* the grave as a *deep six* or *narrow house.* An old expression for burial was being "put to bed with a shovel."

It's often suggested that where the British are death denying, Americans are death defying—and this attitude extends to vocabulary. The British *undertaker's* is the American *funeral parlor* (with, given the ongoing attraction to embalming, associations to beauty parlor); the English *laying-out room* is the *reposing* or *slumber room* in the U.S. The euphemism for embalming is *hygienic treatment* or *temporary preservation;* ashes are *cremains* (cremated remains); a death certificate is a *vital statistics form;* and a hearse is a *casket coach.* It might be fairer to think that such expressions are used just because the funeral business uses them, and that the funeral business uses them to soften the harshness of loss—but it's hard to believe that referring to the cost of the casket as the "amount of investment in the service," or the total price of a funeral as the overall price of "grief therapy," is anything other than a trick of the trade.

Such primness of funerary expression is in stark

contrast with America's love of hard-nosed slang, the argot of Dashiell Hammett, Raymond Chandler, and Elmore Leonard, where death is *the big one* or *the big sleep,* where people get *blown down, chilled, sawed, polished,* or *blipped off, rubbed out, sent West* and *taken for a ride* by *hitmen, trigger men, hatchet men, apaches,* and *torpedoes*—and *put into Chicago over-coats* or *wooden kimonos.* But slang is generally insular, incomprehensible outside its milieu—and short-lived. In current street slang, death is *last out,* dying is *making a deposit* (in the body bank), and someone re-cently deceased or under threat of death is a *sidewalk outline.* Street-talk metaphors don't strive for literary ef-fect—an allusion to death in the vein of Tennyson's "crossing the bar," Pope's "Hell's grim Tyrant" or Byron's "in the dark union of insensate dust" might get someone blipped off or sidewalk-outlined.

 ## Last Words . . . Maybe

You have to be suspicious about the dying utterances of the famous. Did they really say what it's said they said? Did the witnesses have pen and paper? Were they within earshot at the execution? Did those at the bedside, mindful of what might have been more appro-priate, translate the delirious "I want my teeth in" into something like "If humankind doesn't become more ecologically aware the planet is heading for destruction"? It doesn't inspire confidence that many of the dying have more than one set of last words attributed to them. Rabelais has five; the most quoted is "Bring down the curtain, the farce is played out," suspiciously echoed in Beethoven's "Friends, applaud, the comedy is over" (you might, or might not, prefer a Beethoven alternative, "I shall hear in heaven"). And there are other questions: Did the dying deliberately try to think of something memorable, or did it just happen? In either case, did they then shut up so as not to spoil it for posterity?

But some things have to be true, or should be: Caesar's betrayed "Et tu, Brute"; Raleigh's unafraid "Strike, man, strike!"; South Pole explorer Captain Oates's understated "I'm going outside and may be some time." And what of the words of witty men— surely they must be true, for they draw death's string for the rest of us. Voltaire, embodiment of eighteenth-century enlightenment as the bedside lamp flared up: "What? The flames already?" Economic thinker Adam Smith: "I believe we must adjourn this meeting to some other place." Prime Minister Lord Palmerston: "Die my dear doctor? That's the last thing I shall do!" Prime Minister Benjamin Disraeli, whom Queen Victoria proposed to visit: "Why should I see her? She will only want me to give a message to Albert." Irish novelist and carouser Brendan Behan to the nursing nun attending him: "Bless you, sister. May all your sons be bishops."

Wit isn't the sole preserve of the famous. Goethe's not-famous mother, when brought an invitation to a party by a servant girl: "Say Frau Goethe is unable to come, she is busy dying at the moment." Perhaps the remark was feverish rather than deliberately wry. No matter; other final words may have been. King George V's "Bugger Bognor!" Lady Astor's "Am I dying or is this my birthday?" Tallulah Bankhead's "Codeine . . . bourbon." Isn't there something uplifting about showman

LAST words we believe in because we've read them or heard them delivered: "The rest is silence." "A horse! A horse! My kingdom for a horse." "It is a far, far better thing that I do, than I have ever done: it is a far, far better rest that I go to, than I have ever known." "Mother of Mercy! Is this the end of Rico?" "Rosebud." "Made it, Ma! Top of the world!" "Prove it."

Sources, if you don't know or can't remember: *Hamlet; Richard III; A Tale of Two Cities; Little Caesar* (Edward G. Robinson); *Citizen Kane* (Orson Welles); *White Heat* (James Cagney); *Shane* (Jack Palance).

Florenz Ziegfeld's "Curtain! Fast music! Lights! Ready for the last finale! The show looks good. The show looks good"? You can't help smiling, either, in learning that the last thing H. G. Wells said was "I'm all right" and Douglas Fairbanks Jr., "Never better." What better than to be optimistic that the show will go on until the very moment the lights go out? There's something humorous and uplifting, too, in someone's last utterance somehow capturing the essence of the way they've lived. Archimedes, the leading mathematician of the Hellenistic Age, killed by a Roman soldier in the siege of Syracuse: "Wait till I've finished my problem!" The German philosopher Hegel, known for his obscurity: "Only one man understood me, and he didn't understand me." The Russian novelist Tolstoy, who rejected the formal teaching of the Orthodox Church: "Even in the valley of the shadow of death, two and two do not make six." His fellow novelist, the fastidious Frenchman Gide: "I am afraid my sentences are becoming grammatically incorrect."

A doctor who attended five hundred deathbeds said he'd never heard a single memorable word. Even the famous can be banal: Johnson ("I am about to die"), Kant ("Enough"), Byron ("Good night"); nothing is more likely than if death comes suddenly (FDR: "I have a terrible headache"). Perhaps like most people, many of the great minds have been concentrating on the business in hand—or perhaps they didn't see the need. Marx certainly didn't. "Go on, get out!" he yelled at his housekeeper, who'd foolishly asked if he had any last words. "Last words are for fools who haven't said enough!"

If you're keen to say something memorable, it's never too soon to start thinking about it—nobody said last words have to be ex tempore. And you don't want to be taken short like the Mexican bandit Pancho Villa, who, as he lay dying from gunshot wounds, begged newspaper reporters: "Don't let it end like this. Tell them I said something." If you can't think of anything, don't worry. The probability is you'll be sedated anyway.

 ## Goodwill, Ill Will

> *I have nothing. I owe much. The rest I leave to the poor.*
>
> —*Will of François Rabelais (1553)*

Elite Romans had a valid will for most of their lives and changed it frequently, very often on their deathbed. Will making on the deathbed was usual in medieval Europe. The practice petered out in the nineteenth century, which was just as well: at a time when the mind was unlikely to be focused and the emotions were likely to

THE oldest known will was written in 2550 B.C.

be unstable, hasty decisions were possible. The absence of a loved one from the bedside, for example, however valid the reason, could be taken for indifference, with unfortunate results.

The psychology of disinheritance is intriguing, always involving a perceived wrong: not following Dad into the family business, marrying someone disapproved of, infidelity. Most wills are made only with concern for those left behind, but some are payback time, as many young serial wives of very rich old men seem routinely to discover. Other wills that have no vindictive intent but that impose draconian restrictions are made by people, psychologists say, who want to exercise control from beyond the grave or who can't quite believe that the world will function in their absence.

The reading of a will, once a solemn affair, remains a matter of high drama in film and fiction: the covetous relatives on the edge of their chairs in the lawyer's office, whose salivating anticipation turns to fury on discovery that everything's gone to a busty little blonde set up in a place in the city.

In cases where really serious money is involved and those who anticipate receiving it don't, the will is likely to be contested, more often than not on the grounds of the deceased's mental competence—what lawyers call "testamentary capacity." Such lawsuits tend to bring piles of dirty laundry to the courtroom for churning in the media washing machine. When Frank Sinatra died in 1998, he ensured that didn't happen by inserting an unusual "no contest" clause; any heirs who felt miffed over their share were entitled to go to court, but if they did and lost, they would automatically disinherit themselves completely. Ol' Blue Eyes was still singing "My Way." In fact, only about 3 percent of wills come before the courts, and fewer than one in five contests are successful.

Celebrity cases have been less frequent in recent years; arguments over division of the spoils have shifted to the prenuptial agreement. But they still occur, as in the case of a retired investor—and heavy smoker—who left most of the $1.9 million portfolio he'd amassed from investments in tobacco companies to the Canadian Cancer Society, just to spite his family. When his will was contested, the society, to protect its legacy, challenged the contest. In another case, a testator bequeathed a considerable sum to her employer, a local library, on the condition that actor Charles Bronson—whom she'd never met—accepted a gift of

ANNA Nicole Smith, who married an 89-year-old oil billionaire when she was 26, was awarded $88 million of her late husband's estate in March 2002 after a California judge ruled that theirs was a love match. The former stripper and *Playboy* centerfold had been left out of J. Howard Marshall's will in 1995, but the judge ruled that Marshall's son had controlled his father's access to money to deny Smith, and had lied and falsified documents.

$290,000. The testator's mother tried to keep the money in the family, but the library went to court to hold on to what it was to receive.

Few men go to the grave with the sense of self-loathing felt by Michael Henchard, Hardy's mayor of Casterbridge, whose will stipulated that the woman he'd thought to be his daughter wasn't to be told of his death; that nobody was to see his dead body; that he wasn't to be buried in consecrated ground; that there were to be no mourners, no flowers, no tolling bell; and

BILL Adler's book *The Last Will and Testament of Jacqueline Kennedy Onassis* features a photocopy of the entire will "for people who could not afford to buy a piece of Jackie at Sotheby's."

that nobody was to remember his name. But some husbands go with a sliver of ice in their hearts. In 1788 an Englishman called David Davis left his wife five shillings to "enable her to get drunk for the last time at my expense"—echoed almost a hundred years later in Australia, where Francis Lord left his wife a shilling "for the tram fare so she can go somewhere and drown herself." In 1960 Samuel Brett, whose wife wouldn't let him smoke, left her $330,000—on condition she puffed five cigars a day. In 1856 poet and essayist Heinrich Heine left his estate to his wife on condition she remarried so "there will be at least one man to regret my death," but he was probably joking. Not many wives are in a position posthumously to flip off their husbands, but Mrs. Amy Backman was one. When she died in 1959, her will left $600,000 to Bingo, her dog—and $1 to Mr. Backman. Sons-in-law are not always fathers' favorite family additions, but one testator disliked his so much, he left money in a fund for anyone who wanted to sue or assist in any criminal prosecution against him. Whether mildly malicious or just humorous, a doctor left a bequest to one of his sisters "because no one is likely to marry her" and to another "to console her for marrying a man she is obliged to henpeck." Malicious or humorous? A scholar left his nephew "ten thousand, which he will find in a package in my safe." The package turned out to contain ten thousand chess problems. Checkmate.

More wills attest to the individuality and oddity of humankind than to its capacity for malice or humor. In 1927 the Marquis Maurice d'Urre of Aubais left his great estate to the French government on condition that "I wish to be seated in an armchair under a glass dome. This dome must be placed facing the sea in a public place, near a lighthouse and a radio station, and must be perpetually illuminated." During the course of the 1990s in Britain a man left a large sum to a theater, provided his skull was used in *Hamlet*. Another stipulated that the inheritance he bequeathed was on condition that his ashes went into an egg timer, "so that I shall continue to be of use after my death." A woman who believed in vampires left clear instructions that a steel stake was to be driven through her heart. Some people take the will of God literally. In Britain a man left

 FEW women made wills, because property was mostly owned by men, but when they did, in the seventeenth and eighteenth centuries, it was to pass on their clothes—bodices and petticoats, just as much as dresses, ball gowns, and riding suits, were valuable and coveted items.

TEN films with a take on death: *It's a Wonderful Life* (1946)—the ultimate feel-good movie about a man (James Stewart) who wants to end it all on Christmas Eve but who embraces life after seeing what his town would have been like had he never been, thanks to Clarence the middle-aged angel; *Michael* (1996)—lots of films have angels, but not a beer-swilling, womanizing young(ish) slob like Michael (John Travolta); *A Matter of Life and Death* (1946)—heaven as a kind of misty football stadium in which a will-he-won't-he-die wartime pilot (David Niven) argues his case before a celestial jury to be allowed to live; *Ghost* (1990)—schmaltzy but entertaining tale of a stockbroker (Patrick Swayze) killed in a botched mugging who hunts down his killers and saves his wife (Demi Moore) from danger; *Truly Madly Deeply* (1990)—another Dead White Male (Alan Rickman) back in spectral form to help his woman (Juliet Stevenson) come to terms with the pain of loss and learn to let go; *Beetlejuice* (1988)—a newly dead couple try to scare away the new owners of their New England farmhouse and have to get a scarier ghost to help (Alec Baldwin, Geena Davis, Michael Keaton); *High Plains Drifter* (1972)—not just another Clint Eastwood revenge Western, because the town (soon to be renamed Hell) into which he rides has already hanged him; *Devil's Advocate* (1997)— a hotshot young lawyer (Keanu Reeves), unaware of the literalness of the title, joins a big law firm run by Al Pacino overacting as you know who; *The Sixth Sense* (1999)—encounter of a child psychologist (Bruce Willis) with a boy (unnervingly well played by Haley Joel Osment) who sees dead people; *The Son's Room* (2001)—

tender Italian story of a couple's feelings when their son dies young, which doesn't indulge in Catholic angst and lifts the gloom with a lightness of touch.

£26,000 to Jesus, if his identity could be established. In the United States a woman left part of her estate to God. When the will was filed, the local sheriff solemnly reported that "after due and diligent search, God cannot be found in Cherokee County."

The complete wills of many of the famous can be found these days on various websites—everyone from Elvis to Princess Di. Most run to many, many pages. But length doesn't necessarily make a will watertight. One 148-page, closely written document was recently declared invalid—though that had less to do with length than with the fact that there was an argument as to why the deceased's entire estate should be used to build a mausoleum for him and his dog. Brevity isn't a bar to validity; the shortest will known (Vse zene—"everything to my wife"), made in 1967, was declared in order, as was the twenty-three-worder of U.S. president Calvin Coolidge: "Not unmindful of my son, I give all of my estate, both real and personal, to my wife, Grace Coolidge." Chief Justice Edward Douglass White wrote a fifty-one-word will also leaving everything to his widow that was such a model of concision and clarity that it was published in textbooks. One layman clipped it out, and added "My wishes are the same as Justice White's," and signed it. A difficulty at law arose: did the deceased intend to benefit his own widow or Mrs. White?

For many Americans, like ancient Romans, the law is an everyday tool, and yet 40 percent have no will, including 30 percent of those over fifty-five. In Britain in 2001, fifty-three thousand—almost 10 percent of the population—died intestate. Even when people do make wills, some seem reluctant to leave them with lawyers or banks or put them in deposit boxes for safekeeping— wills are still found under mattresses, in the pages of books, or in the glove compartments or trunks of cars. Is it carelessness? Not usually, apparently. The reason wills are either not written or are given only a kind of "unofficial" status through hiding them or leaving them carelessly about is superstition. Many see making a will as tempting providence—an implication that they're ready to turn their life's last page.

 ## Obits: The Smallest Biographies

News of Mark Twain's death in 1897 came as a surprise to his alter ego Sam Clemens: he was on a lecture tour in Europe at the time. Twain telegramed the editor

MAJOR General Frank Richardson, who has died aged 92, was awarded a Distinguished Service Order in Eritrea, became a champion bagpipe player, and was the author of *Mars without Venus: A study of some homosexual generals.—Daily Telegraph* obituary notice

who'd printed his obituary: "The report of my death was an exaggeration" (not, note in passing, the usually quoted "greatly exaggerated").

Other men have also had the eerie experience of seeing their obituaries in print while they're still breathing, including former Russian president Boris Yeltsin (though it's a pinch of salt to a pile of rubles that he was too zonked on vodka to know anything about it). Another was the Swedish chemist Alfred Nobel, and the experience changed his life. Twain's inopportune obit stemmed from confusion following the death of a cousin, Nobel's from the death of his brother. Nobel, the inventor of dynamite, was shocked to read of himself as the "dynamite king," without any consideration given to his intention of breaking down the barriers that separated men. He pondered the purpose of his life— and in his will left an endowment for the foundation of the Nobel peace prize (as well as five other annual

BOOKS on dying well, such as the Egyptian and Tibetan books of the dead, have existed throughout history. In medieval times the instructional cycle of texts known as *Ars Moriendi* was translated into nearly every European language and had a huge influence on European thought for two hundred years.

In the Victorian period even children's literature was given over to the subject of death. The 1824 *Child's Companion* cheerfully informed: "You may not live to see the end of the year just begun. How many little graves you see in the churchyard."

Since the 1991 publication of Derek Humphry's best seller *Final Exit,* a manual of practical advice on how to commit suicide, books on death have been a growth industry. The Natural Death Centre (www.naturaldeath.org.uk) offers *The New Natural Death Handbook,* which contains everything you could possibly want to know about death in the U.K., from coffin buying to NDEs. Jessica Mitford's *The American Way of Death Revisited* is available in an edition updated just before her own last good-bye.

awards in physics, chemistry, physiology or medicine, and literature), a cause that lived up to his name.

The obituary came into its own in the nineteenth century. In the eighteenth, when the daily and weekly newspapers were read in London's coffeehouses, the pages were few, and any valedictions were only of the mighty. These were lengthy encomiums—not unlike biographies of that era, which Abraham Lincoln refused to read because, he said, they "are not only misleading but false . . . making a wonderful hero of their subject . . . magnifies his perfections—if he has any—and suppresses his imperfections." In the nineteenth century the steam printing press arrived, and in a proliferating newspaper market (a staggering thirty million copies a day in Britain) the obit not only broadened its scope but took the opportunity, on occasion, to pepper some departed backsides with buckshot. The nature of the obit changed in other ways. Where previously the lofty intention was to record the actions of the departed and set them in the context of the age, now it tried to catch the personality, warts and all.

Some journalists assigned to the obituary-writing department have traditionally referred to it as the "graveyard," but turning out a living portrait of the dead in a limited number of words can be a skill and even an art. The job also has power—not everyone gets the chance to slip a knife between the ribs of a reputation. The last writes indeed—dead men can't sue. Such power came in for some gentle ribbing from Mark Twain some years after the untimely report of his death:

Of necessity, an Obituary is a thing which cannot be so judiciously edited by any hand as by that of

ELEVEN novels in which death isn't just an incident but a "character": *Under the Volcano* (Malcolm Lowry)—on the Day of the Dead in Mexico a brilliant, chaotically minded drunk moves inexorably to his end; *The Third Policeman* (Flann O'Brien)—a farcical, very Irish murder story in which the narrator is dead throughout in a deserved kind of hell; *Epitaph of a Small Winner* (Machado de Assis)—life story of a philosophic hedonist, funny but pessimistic; *Malone Dies* (Samuel Beckett)—deathbed soliloquy of an old and helpless man; *The Spire* (William Golding)—the building on a medieval cathedral of a spire whose shadow falls darkly on the man who thought God had chosen him to do the job; *Brighton Rock* (Graham Greene)—an action thriller ("Hale knew they meant to murder him before he had been in Brighton three hours") that is also an examination of evil personified in the boy psycho Pinkie; *Lolita* (Vladimir Nabokov)—jail cell confession of the nymphet-obsessed Humbert Humbert, whose inefficient shooting of his rival Quigley is one of the blackest comic scenes in fiction; *The Great Gatsby* (F. Scott Fitzgerald)—a morality tale of the emptiness of riches involving a hit-and-run death, a murder, a suicide, and a funeral that almost nobody attends; *The Blood of the Lamb* (Peter De Vries)—typically funny, but tear-inducing death of a child that her father will never come to terms with; *The Death of Vishnu* (Manil Suri)—an odd-job man dying on the staircase of a Bombay apartment building looks back over his life; *Last Orders* (Graham Swift)—rite of passage for four men on the way to the coast to scatter the ashes of an old friend in the sea.

ACCORDING to Salman Rushdie, "We can best understand the nature of this culture if we say that it found its truest mirror in a corpse"—which is as good a description of the cult of the celebrity dead as you'll get.

The twentieth century wasn't the first to sanctify the departed famous, but access to mass media made it into a worldwide phenomenon. The list of secular gods and goddesses stretches from Rudolph Valentino to James Dean, Eva Perón, Marilyn Monroe, JFK and Jackie O, Elvis Presley, John Lennon—and Princess Diana. Lennon's sardonic comment that the Beatles were "more popular than Jesus" might have gone further: for some people the celebrity dead have virtually replaced Jesus.

Elvis remains the world's most famous dead person, but Princess Di, the world's most famous living person before her death, might be challenging for his title—and for deification. Her burial on an island in the middle of a lake on the Althorp estate in Northamptonshire at the very least makes her a figure of contemporaneous Arthurian legend.

Some evangelical Christians see the reaction to Diana's death as part of the fledgling spiritual revival of Britain; others are less keen. "We should be careful that she is not worshipped," said the archbishop of York, David Hope. For the moment Diana remains "God's newest angel," as one of the floral tributes outside Kensington Palace called her, a saint in waiting—the patron saint of bulimia, perhaps. As yet no one has written books, as they have of Elvis, claiming that she's been in touch from the other side. No one has claimed, as they have of Elvis, that she's left messages on their answering machine. There have been no worldwide sightings, as there have of Elvis. And yet that mightn't be true. A "vision" of Diana was seen by a number of mourners who'd waited in line for up to eleven hours to sign the books of condolence at Kensington. Diana's face, they said, looked out from a painting at the end of the hall. . . .

the subject of it. In such a work it is not the Facts that are of chief importance, but the light which the obituarist shall throw upon them, the meaning which he shall dress them in, the conclusions which he shall draw from them, and the judgements which he shall deliver upon them. The Verdicts, you understand: that is the danger-line.

Twain proposed that every paper holding obituaries of him should send him copies and he would correct them—"not the Facts, but the Verdicts"—so that when he got to "the Other Side, where there are some who are not friendly to me," he could make a favorable impression. Without doubt the idea would find favor among many potential obituary subjects, but would take the fun out of reading their obituaries. People do like reading obituaries, even of those they don't know.

Some read obituaries, as the old joke goes, to check on whether they're still alive; others for the satisfaction of seeing that their enemies aren't. As the American civil liberties lawyer Clarence Darrow once said: "I never wanted to see anybody die, but there are a few obituary notices I have read with pleasure."

Run-of-the-mill obits are still, as media analyst George Gerbner called them, "social registers of the middle class," and the interesting wrinkles are frequently botoxed out. As in the eulogy, few people aren't better people in their life summary than they were in life. When the lightheartedly cynical short-story writer Saki (H. H. Munro) said of someone, "He is one of those people who would be enormously improved by death," he meant something else, but the point holds good. Obit photos enormously improve the dead, too, because they're inevitably pure Dorian Gray, showing their subjects in their prime, not the crumblies they'd probably become. It's almost worth dying to look that good again.

 ## The Epitaph: Final, Final Words

Some people write their own epitaph; most are written by others. The poet Keats wanted simply "Here lies One Whose Name was writ in Water," but ahead of this line

TEN novels with death in the title: *Death in Venice* (Thomas Mann), *Death on the Installment Plan* (Céline), *Death in the Afternoon* (Ernest Hemingway), *Death of the Heart* (Elizabeth Bowen), *As I Lay Dying* (William Faulkner), *Veronica Decides to Die* (Paulo Coelho), *A Lesson Before Dying* (Ernest J. Gaines), *The Lake of Dead Languages* (Carol Goodman), *Dead Famous* (Ben Elton), *Being Dead* (James Crace).

he got "This Grave contains all that was Mortal of a Young English Poet Who on his Death Bed in the Bitterness of his Heart at the Malicious Power of his enemies Desires these words to be engraved on his Tomb Stone." Keats's works had been mocked in his lifetime, but he wanted nothing of the sort; the well-meaning can make the dead look like pretentious prats forevermore. As the seventeenth-century essayist Joseph Addison noted after spending an afternoon amusing himself with the inscriptions on the tombs in Westminster Abbey: "Some of them were covered with such extravagant epitaphs that, if it were possible for the dead person to be acquainted with them, he would blush at the praises which his friends have bestowed upon him."

Ancient Greek epitaphs were often tender, expressive, epigrammatic, and usually in elegiac verse, as, for example, "Go tell the Spartans, thou that passest by / That here, obedient to their laws, we lie"—reflected in the common eighteenth-century inscription, "Beware ye who passing by / As ye be now so once was I / As I be now so must ye be / Prepare for death and follow me." The more rigorous Romans, like the Egyptians before them, as a rule recorded only the facts and often added a warning not to desecrate the grave, as later, among others, did Shakespeare's (not thought to be by the bardic hand): "Good friend for Jesus sake forebeare / To digg the dust encloased heare! / Blest be the man that spares thes stones / And curst be he that moves my bones." Common on the grave of Roman cynics were the initials NF.F.NS.NC, standing for *Non furi, furi, non sum, non curo:* "I was not. I was. I am not. I care not."

For many centuries Latin was the preferred language for epitaphs. The earliest in English churches usually include the phrase *hic jacet,* "here lies." The French that superseded it in the thirteenth century was itself overtaken in the fourteenth by English, but even three hundred years later the educated stuck to Latin or Greek. Samuel Johnson refused to write an English epitaph for Oliver Goldsmith because, he said, it would disgrace the walls of Westminster Abbey. Rather than see the use of the classical as intellectual snobbery, the kindly

CEMETERIES and churchyards were once referred to as "God's acre," borrowing from a German, not a Saxon phrase, as wrongly attributed by the poet Longfellow.

Addison put the practice down to an attempt at "excessive modesty" on the internees' behalf, though, he observed, such inscriptions "are not understood once in a twelvemonth."

Until the seventeenth century epitaphs were affordable only to the elite. With the rise of the middle class in the next two hundred years, a fitting postmortem inscription became de rigueur. Most had at least one eye on respectability and social standing—so much so that Charles Lamb wondered, "Where are all the bad people buried?" But the clever epitaph abounded in acrostics, riddles, palindromes, and puns on names and professions. In one of his lighter moments Benjamin Franklin penned his own epitaph, playing on his former trade: "The Body of B. Franklin, Printer / Like the cover of an old Book / Its Contents torn out and Stript of its Lettering & Guilding / Lies here, food for Worms / But the work shall not be wholly lost / for it will, as he believed, appear once more / In a new and more Elegant Edition / corrected and amended / By the Author." The epitaph of an English blacksmith made similar play: "His sledge and hammer lie reclin'd / His bellows too have lost their wind / His fire's extinct, his forge decayed / His vice all in the dust is laid / His coal is spent, his iron gone / His last nail's driven, his work is done." So did that of a clock and watchmaker "who departed this life wound up in hope of being taken in hand by his Maker and being thoroughly cleaned, repaired and set agoing in the world to come." So too that of a lawyer who was "so great a lover of peace that when a contention arose between life and death he immediately yielded up the ghost to end the dispute." A satiric inversion of the common Greek epitaph "may the earth lie light on thee" was erected over Sir John Vanbrugh, architect of many English great houses: "Lie heavy on him, Earth! for he / Laid many heavy loads on thee."

THE eighteenth-century British printer and typographer John Baskerville—the typeface bearing his name is still popular—was an atheist who chose to be buried in unconsecrated ground, and had a cone rather than a stone or cross put over him, bearing the words: "May the example contribute to emancipate thy mind from the idle fears of SUPERSTITION and the wicked arts of priesthood." The cone was soon overturned and "the remains of the man himself desecrated."

British and American tombstone inscriptions might have been expected to display nothing but solemnity, but our forebears had learned to live in close proximity with Death in a way we no longer experience; if they didn't exactly look on him as a friend, they at least expected him to be able to take a joke. "Life is a jest, and all things show it / I thought so once, and now I know it"—the poet John Gay was another who wrote his own epitaph. The cast of mind wasn't unusual: "Here lie I by the chancel door / they put me here because I was poor / The further in, the more you pay / But here I lie as snug as they"; "Here lie I, Martin Elginbrod / Have mercy on my soul, Lord God / As I on you, were I Lord God / And you were Martin Elginbrod."

Some names cried out for the punny epitaph. The antiquary Thomas Fuller went to his grave under "Fuller's Earth," a Mr. Shallow was laid in a Deep Grave, a Mrs. Nott was "Nott Alive and is Nott Dead," and the stone above a certain Thorpe said only, "Thorpe's

THE inscription on the grave of a Wells Fargo agent who had been shot in an argument over a consignment in Tombstone, Arizona, couldn't be more succinct: "Here lies / Lester Moore / four slugs / from a .44 / no less / no more."

corpse." When a centenarian called Young died, it was almost inevitable that he "died Young," though someone even older gets a bigger laugh: "Here Lyes Stephen Rumbold / He lived to ye Age of 100 & 1 / Sanguine & Strong / An hundred to one / You don't Live so Long."

Some epitaphs are unintentionally funny: "Sacred to the memory of / Captain Anthony Wedgwood / Accidentally shot by his gamekeeper / Whilst out shooting / Well done thou good and faithful servant"; "Erected to the memory of / John McFarlane / Drown'd in the Water of Leith / By a few affectionate friends." Other epitaphs bring a smile because of their simplicity ("Here lies John Taggart of honest fame / of stature low & a leg lame / Content was he with a portion small / kept a shop in Wigtown and that's all") or their fortitude ("Nathaniel Hawthorne / Poorly lived / And poorly died / Poorly buried / And no one cried"). Yet others bring a smile that may hide a tear: "Here lie two babbies, dead as nits / Who died in agonising fitts / They were too good to live with we / So God did take to live with He"; "Here lies father and mother and sister and I / We all died within the space of one short year / They all be buried at Wimble, except I / And I be buried here." And this, on a victim of the resurrection men: "Her body dissected by fiendish men / Her bones anatomised / Her soul we trust has risen to God / A place where few physicians rise."

There's anger in that, and in this: "Donald Robertson / He was a peaceable quiet man, and to all / appearances a sincere Christian / His death was very much regretted / which was caused by the stupidity of Lawrence Tulloch of Clotherton / who sold him nitre instead of Epsom salts by which he was killed in the space of / three hours after taking a dose of it." And this: "Ellen Shannon / Who was fatally burned / March 21st 1870 / by an explosion of a lamp / filled with R. E. Danforth's / Non Explosive / Burning Fluid." There's anger in the following, but you can't help laughing, and being intrigued at what lies behind it, and wondering why there haven't been many more of its kind: "Here Lieth / Mary, the wife of John Ford / We hope her soul is / Gone to the Lord / But if for hell she / has changed this life / She had better be there / Than be John Ford's wife."

All the epitaphs here have been verified; many oth-

MANY epitaphs have copied lines of poetry, perhaps the most popular source being Thomas Gray's "An Elegy Written in a Country Church-yard." The most noted modern epitaph was written by William Butler Yeats for himself: "Cast a cold eye / On life, on death / Horseman, pass by!"

ers that are frequently quoted have probably never appeared on gravestones—though the evidence decays or gets broken up by local councils for use in road paving, so who knows? The humorist Fritz Spiegl traced a number of them to the eighteenth-century *The Epitaph Writer: Consisting of Upwards of Six Hundred Original Epitaphs, Moral, Admonitory, Humorous and Satirical,* from which this is an example: "Here lies a lewd Fellow, who, while he / drew Breath / in the Midst of his Life was in Quest of his / Death / Which he quickly obtain'd for it cost him / his Life / For being in Bed with another man's Wife." Sadly, this too is almost certainly apocryphal: "Here lie the bones of Elizabeth Charlotte / Born a virgin, died a harlot / She was aye a virgin at seventeen / a remarkable thing in Aberdeen." And this: "Here lies Jamie Smith, wife of Thomas Smith,

SOME brief celebrity inscriptions that seem to capture the essence of those beneath them: "I never met a man I didn't like" (Will Rogers); "That's all, folks!" (Mel Blanc); "She did it the hard way" (Bette Davis); "Everybody loves somebody sometime" (Dean Martin). And you can't help warming to Busby Berkeley, whose epitaph makes no reference to choreography or kaleidoscopes of chorus girls but to what in the final analysis he must have been proudest of: "2nd Lt U.S. Army / World War 1."

marble cutter / This monument was erected by her husband as a tribute to her memory / and a specimen of his work / Monuments of the same style 350 dollars." But wouldn't you like to believe that somewhere there's a tombstone inscribed "Beneath this sod lies another"?

The art of the epitaph is lost, or out of favor. The British seem content with a handful of phrases such as "gone to sleep," "reunited at last," "a wonderful wife and mother," "the best dad in the world"—the walls of heaven could be papered with them. Americans in many places have replaced tombstones with grave plaques, which are Romanesque in their brevity.

Name, date in, and date out may be little enough to mark a life, as so many inscriptions now do. Yet in the case of W. C. Fields (1880–1946) it seems absolutely appropriate. What could be more misanthropic? Actually, in 1925 Fields did write an epitaph for *Vanity Fair* that read: "I would rather be living in Philadelphia," but it didn't make it to his final resting place. It's a shame his dying words to his longtime lover didn't either: "God damn the whole friggin' world and everyone in it but you, Carlotta." Now *that's* an epitaph.

AFTERWORD

 Has Death Got a Future?

All my possessions for a moment of time.
— *Last words of Queen Elizabeth I*

Thomas Parr of Shropshire, England, married for the first time when he was eighty, was caught out in adultery twenty-five years later—and compelled to stand in church clad in a white sheet as penance—then remarried at 112, to the stated satisfaction of his second wife, and lived another forty years. Brought to London by the earl of Arundel as a curiosity, he succumbed to the "generous rich and varied diet, and strong drink." He was interred in Westminster Abbey.

*THO. PARR OF YE COUNTY OF SALLOP.
BORNE IN AD: 1483. HE LIVED IN YE REIGNES
OF TEN PRINCES VIZ: K.EDW.4. K.EDW.5.
K.RICH.3. K.HEN.7. K.HEN.8. K.EDW.6. Q.MA.
Q.ELIZ. K.JA. & K.CHARLES. AGED 152
YEARES & WAS BURYED HERE NOVEMB. 15.
1635.*

In a churchyard near Cardiff the tombstone of William
Edwards of Cacreg, buried thirty-three years after Parr,
claims that he was 168. It may be true. Given men's
competitiveness and inclination to boast about length,
it probably isn't; at 152 Parr is the oldest verifiable
human being who has lived. And however much life averages have expanded, we're still mostly checking out
at about half his age. But we live in interesting times.
Alchemy never did find out how to turn base metal into
gold, but that other quest of the ages, the search for the
elixir of life, may soon triumph. Hormone injections can
slow the body's rundown, stem cell research is leading
inexorably to the cloning of tissue and organs, and the
recently identified longevity gene—which all centenarians have and most people don't—will become available just as soon as science works out its exact DNA
sequence. By 2050 biological immortality could be
yours.

Well, perhaps not immortality—though who knows where nanotechnological regeneration, robotic supplementation, and even, on the wilder side, the downloading of the mind onto hard drive, may lead. We're within spitting distance of achieving average life expectancy of 100 (by 2020, according to at least one respected futurologist); others predict we'll be getting on a Parr with old Tho, or even go beyond him to 180 or 200—and healthily, science emphasizes, because biotechnology and genetic engineering offer the tantalizing prospect of eliminating genetically borne disease. It could be that those entering the life cycle in the first decade of the twenty-first century will see the dawn of the twenty-second, or even get halfway to the twenty-third. If so, it's going to get crowded down here. The world population of six billion is estimated to reach ten billion in fifty years even without taking into account all those golden oldies skipping around singing "I'm going to live forever."

But however humankind pushes the envelope, the Moving Finger must eventually write, or more likely tap out on its keyboard, THE END, and we'll have to move on. Will, then, 100, 150, 200, seem enough? Perhaps you'll be prepared like Peter Pan to say: "To die will be an awfully big adventure." Perhaps you'll go with a philosophical shrug, in agreement with Montaigne, who was ready to "make room for others, as others have done for you." Perhaps, in the words of the Dylan Thomas poem, you'll "rage, rage against the dying of the light"—and go kicking and screaming.

However you do it, have a safe journey.

INDEX

ABOUT THE AUTHOR

Tom Hickman is a writer and journalist now living on the Sussex coast of England. His other books include *What Did You Do in the War, Auntie?,* the story of the BBC during World War II, and *The Sexual Century,* made into a Carlton TV series.